Living the
Feminist Dream

Living the Feminist Dream

A Faithful Vision for Women in the Church and the World

Kate Bryan

New City Press
Hyde Park, New York

Published by New City Press
202 Comforter Blvd.,
Hyde Park, NY 12538
www.newcitypress.com

Living the Feminist Dream
A Faithful Vision for Women in the Church and the World

Kate Bryan

Cover design and layout by Miguel Tejerina

Library of Congress Control Number: 2021919422

ISBN 978-1-56548-516-7 (paperback)
ISBN 978-1-56548-518-1 (e-book)
Printed in the United States of America

Contents

Series Preface

Does the book that you are about to read seem unusual? Perhaps even counterintuitive?

Good. The Magenta series wouldn't be doing its job if you felt otherwise.

On the color wheel, magenta lies directly between red and blue. Just so, books in this series do not lie at one limit or another of our hopelessly simplistic, two-dimensional, antagonistic, binary imagination. Often, in the broader culture any answer to a moral or political question gets labeled as liberal or conservative, red or blue. But the Magenta series refuses to play by these shortsighted rules. Magenta will address the complexity of the issues of our day by resisting a framework that unnecessarily pits one idea against another. Magenta refuses to be defined by anything other than a positive vision of the good.

If you understand anything about the Focolare's dialogical-and-faithful mission, it should not surprise you that this series has found a home with the Focolare's New City Press. The ideas in these books, we believe, will spark dialogues that will heal divides and build unity at the very sites of greatest fragmentation and division.

The ideas in Magenta are crucial not only for our fragmented culture, but also for the Church. Our secular idolatry— our simplistic left/right, red/blue imagination—has oozed into the Church as well, disfiguring the Body of Christ with ugly disunity. Such idolatry, it must be said, has muffled the Gospel and crippled the Church, keeping it from being salt and light in a wounded world desperate for unity.

Magenta is not naïve. We realize full well that appealing to dialogue or common ground can be dismissed as a weak-sauce, milquetoast attempt to cloud our vision of the good or reduce it to a mere least common denominator. We know that much dialogic spade work is yet to be done, but that does not keep the vision of the Magenta Series (like the color it bears) from being *bold*. There is nothing half-hearted about it. All our authors have a brilliant, attractive vision of the good.

And having Kate Bryan's book as our opening volume shows exactly what this series is about. *Living the Feminist Dream* addresses important, neuralgic issues in a characteristically Magenta way: boldly, carefully, dialogically—and by telling lots and lots of stories.

Enjoy!

Charles C. Camosy

Introduction

A couple of years ago, living and working in Washington, DC, I was part of a great group of friends and a good community. My public relations career was thriving. Many perceived that I was "living the dream," and I would agree. I could do what I wanted when I wanted, made good money, and didn't want for anything. Every morning I would wake up, pour a cup of coffee, and in peace read the headlines and major stories in every DC and national newspaper. But one morning everything changed. As I went through my usual routine everything—my beliefs, faith, and all I had worked for, lived for, and fought for—collided. I hit a "suddenly" moment.

That sunny August morning in 2016 I came across an article in the *Washington Post* by a woman who had recently published a book about sexuality. She argued that chastity and abstinence were archaic. She had been raised in a conservative evangelical home and, like so many other young people in the 90's, had read Joshua Harris's infamous book *I Kissed Dating Goodbye*. As a teenager she had taken his advice to abstain from sex before marriage, but as an adult felt that her life and relationships had been damaged by thinking like that and living her life in this way. As I read her piece I understood where she was coming from because in high school I too had read that book and bought into the "Harris creed" concerning love and abstinence. But simultaneously I felt disheartened because unlike the *WaPo* author—who was being touted as an expert—my understanding had evolved since high school. I had come to recognize chastity as the "perfection of love," and living this way had led me to true freedom. Instead of evolving, her understanding had been shackled. She had not gone beyond what she learned as a high schooler and blamed chastity for what had happened, or not happened, throughout her life. Instead of recognizing value in how she'd been raised and how she lived her life, she dismissed it. She felt bitterness and regret about her upbringing and wanted to tell the world about it.

That same morning I read another article, by a different author, with a similar thesis. She had also saved sex for marriage, got married young, had a couple of kids, found herself exhausted, and now seemed very unhappy. She also blamed her upbringing, presuming that if she had more sexual experiences in her younger years she would have chosen a different path and a different life altogether.

As I read both pieces, I felt compassion for these women. But at the same time I felt unsettled and angry (righteous anger) that no one had led them to a deeper understanding of sexual integrity and relationships. Left to fend for themselves, they did not question what Joshua Harris had preached. And they are not alone. Harris sold 1.2 million copies of *I Kissed Dating Goodbye*. The many young people who bought into this faulty "theology" believed that not kissing and not having sex before marriage would guarantee a free and fulfilled life. They accepted the shackles of Harris's teaching when they could have discovered, as I did, that—when understood fully and correctly—chastity and sexual integrity actually bring true freedom.

There are deeper issues at work here, but ultimately "surface level purity culture" and Christian celebrity culture are problematic. I disagree on many levels with the so-called "chastity" that has been preached in many circles. That understanding falls short, and we've watched the failures play out in modern culture. To me, the underlying issue is consistency—consistency between what you preach and how you live your life, consistency between what you say and who you are. Christian author, podcaster, and female empowerment coach Rachel Hollis came under fire for demeaning her domestic help as someone who "cleans my toilets." Hollis, who so passionately promoted women's dignity and purpose, was caught living in a way that clashed with what she was preaching. Famed Hillsong pastor Carl Lentz regularly preached about life, faith, and following Christ, but it came out that he had been unfaithful to his wife and sexually assaulted numerous women. And then there's Josh Duggar, who was raised in a community that preached "save sex and kissing until marriage," but years later it came out that not only was he unfaithful to his wife, but also during his teenage years he had abused his sisters. He became what many would call a "sex addict," and his computer was filled with child pornography so horrifying that a Department of Homeland Security agent testified it was "in the top five of the worst of the worst that I've ever had to examine." I don't lay all the blame on the surface-level preaching and teaching concerning chastity and faith, but I do partially blame the foundation that has been laid through it, and secondarily I do blame the hypocrisy in figures like Hollis and Lenz and Duggar, and the lack of consistency between what they preach and teach and how they live. And we ourselves, as Christians, may be no different. No one is perfect, but we should always be consistent—or at least strive to be consistent—in everything we say and do.

Years after I *Kissed Dating Goodbye*, Harris and the megachurch where he preached were rocked by a sex abuse scandal. Although Harris is said not to have been involved, he and his wife separated and he has said that he lost his Christian faith. Harris has renounced I *Kissed Dating Goodbye* stating, "I apologized for it. I unpublished the books. I pulled the books off the market. But you can't give people [back], you know, years of their life."

Harris has since gone on to launch an online course to "deconstruct" his teachings and anyone "harmed by purity culture." His course, "Reframe Your Story," includes a $275 "Deconstruction Starter Pack." It's noteworthy that, just as he did before,

Harris is capitalizing off himself, his "celebrity," and more faulty teachings. If you were "harmed by the purity culture," you don't need more Joshua Harris . . . you need someone more qualified to talk to. But this new phase of his career illustrates a pervasive, shallow understanding of chastity. That's one of my motivations for writing this book.

When I heard about Harris leaving his faith behind, my heart hurt for him and for the many who followed him and his teachings—not just because his life was falling apart and so many people had been misled, but because Harris said he lost his faith. From what I know about him and his life—which is definitely not everything—Josh himself seems to have been misled by his own church leaders. By the time he was elevated as a young "expert" and began preaching a faulty understanding of faith and chastity, he was too deep in his "surface level purity theology" to evolve. And the same people that were teaching him and walking with him through his ministry weren't being consistent and faithful to what they were preaching. He got so lost and those who had been leading him ended up exploiting him so much that he lost his faith. Harris's case illustrates why I think that when we don't seek a deeper understanding of theology itself, particularly chastity, and when we tout young people—who haven't even had a chance to grow up—as "leaders" and celebrities, we're missing so much. No one is perfect and everyone is going to fail and fall, but there is definitely a problem when any person is elevated as someone to trust ourselves to unquestioningly—unless we're talking about Jesus. Jesus' mother Mary and the saints are examples to follow and imitate, but even the saints weren't perfect. Most humans will surely fail us, but we should look for the goodness in those around us and emulate their positive qualities. We should never hold other human beings to unattainable standards.

My own experience with faith and my understanding of chastity was different. It could be said that I had better faith teachers growing up. Actually, though, there's something more, something inside. I have always been a "seeker." I have always had strong convictions, but I've also been open to others' viewpoints and sought to understand them in hopes that I would discover the full truth.

Sitting at my kitchen table, processing both articles, I felt many chapters of my life unfolding and connecting—like puzzle pieces coming together. I recognized the legitimacy of these women's stories and perspectives, but my experience told me that so much was missing. My PR career taught me that sometimes someone just needs to pitch another perspective.

I felt frustrated with the authors, but also with the *Washington Post* for presenting only one viewpoint. But I also felt frustrated because it was likely that no one submitted an alternative viewpoint. We often forget—I myself definitely do—that sometimes the onus is on us. Sometimes we blame the publication or the author for not presenting other views—I do, even though I work in media—but I've come to realize that sometimes we have to step up as the person to present that other view. Reach out to the editor or reporter; you never know what will happen. I did, and sure enough something did happen.

A bit of my backstory: I suffered a lot of adversity and bullying growing up, but through it I forged an inner power to live out my integral beliefs. Although my immediate family have always been incredibly supportive, many relatives and others in my life vehemently opposed everything I stood for and would regularly mock me and my beliefs. Those experiences wounded me, but also made me grow deeper and even more steadfast in my faith and in everything that I believed to be true. Such experiences led me to study theology at Franciscan University of Steubenville, where in my thesis I compared the Catholic and the Evangelical understanding of chastity—arguing that the teachings of the Catholic Church convey a full understanding of that virtue. And because of my beliefs, I myself have chosen to live a life of chastity and save sex for marriage. And reading those articles that morning, all those things in my past came into focus.

Sitting at the kitchen table that morning I had a "suddenly" moment. A moment where my entire life seemed to come together and my next step became clear. Someone needed to respond to those articles in the *Washington Post*, and I assure you I didn't want to be that person. I knew full well what it would mean for me to speak so publicly about something I had lived so privately for so many years. But even if no one else wanted to write the piece, I felt convicted to respond, to discuss my decision to live a life of chastity and how that led to my "living the feminist dream." I ended up writing that piece and to everyone's shock and disbelief, including my own, *The Washington Post* ran it. And it went viral.

Moments like that lead us where we're supposed to be. I would even venture to say that every single person we encounter helps us on the life path we are meant to walk. Whether through simple acquaintances or serious relationships, every single person helps us discover who and where we're supposed to be.

Sometimes my life seems like a picture puzzle scattered across the floor. I can't visualize the final image that they add up to, but I continue to gather the pieces. Sometimes an individual piece doesn't seem to fit or doesn't make sense on its own; another might suggest a clue of what is to come. Or as Michael Scott famously said in the US version of *The Office*, "Sometimes I'll start a sentence, and I don't even know where it's going. I just hope I find it along the way. Like an improv conversation. An improversation." Life truly, sometimes feels like an improversation. But in those "suddenly moments," like my experience with the *Washington Post* articles, the puzzle pieces fit together and reveal something we were always meant to be or do.

We are as unique and complex as our fingerprints. People may see us only as a version of ourselves that represents who they think we are and judge us by the neatly labeled box they have put us in, but each of us is complex, multifaceted, and fascinating. We should be consistent in seeing every person as precious, created for a purpose, created in love, created for love.

Women in particular hold a unique purpose and a unique power to change the world. Mary, Jesus' mother, exemplifies such purpose and power. The Blessed Mother—particularly Our Lady of Guadalupe—has become an important part of my daily life. I look to her for inspiration, and when I pray I confide in her just like I would talk to my own mother or another significant woman in my life. In Mary I envision a woman whose life transformed the world. If you know her story, you know that when she was engaged to Joseph and the path of her life seemed to be heading in a certain direction, she was visited by an angel who asked her to give up everything to carry the child Jesus. She said "Yes," a yes that changed the world. Each woman shares in that unique power. We were created for a unique purpose—not just the power to create and carry human life, but the power—no matter what job or life direction we choose—to change the world. But so often that unique purpose and power is overlooked. The world overlooks it; the church overlooks it; we ourselves overlook it.

I wrote this book to share stories that I may never have the opportunity to share anywhere else. I also wrote this book because I believe in the power of stories and I believe that every person—and every person's story—has the power to transform the world. I'll share stories from my own life journey, stories of other women who I admire, and lessons I've learned as I've evolved and grown. My greatest hope is that this book helps you understand your own life in a new way, gives you a different perspective on faith and life, and helps you find purpose and passion. You were created to change the world. Throughout all of history there has never been anyone like you and there never will be anyone like you. The world needs you, now more than ever. The world needs you and who you were created to be! This book will present my unique perspective on faith, life, relationships, and many other things. As I said, I'm definitely a "seeker"; I hope this book encourages you to be a seeker as well. Open your heart and your mind to the others around you; let's find new ways to love one another as we travel this journey through life together. I'm grateful that you are here and I'm excited that you can take me on your journey with you.

Let me conclude this intro with these inspiring words that Pope John Paul II, paraphrasing Catherine of Siena, proclaimed to the million and more young people at World Youth Day 2000:

"If you are what you should be, you will set the whole world ablaze ."

Each of us is on a journey. Some portions we must walk by ourselves; others we can walk together. I want to walk this journey with you, and I hope you'll walk with me through my own life journey. We can recognize that our lives contain the power, purpose, and ability to change the world. To quote one of my other favorite queens, Shania Twain, "Let's go girls!" Let's set the whole world ablaze

Chapter 1

Growing up

I grew up in a small town in Michigan, a midwestern kid. My parents, who never graduated from college, worked incredibly hard to provide a stable life for themselves and for us. They were determined not to repeat their parents' and grandparents' mistakes, and to create a better family life for their kids than they had. My mom was born and raised in a Catholic household; my dad was raised Lutheran but—spoiler alert—he converted to Catholicism when I was sixteen. Being born and raised in a mixed-religion household presented certain advantages and disadvantages, but in fact both sides of the family were very much alike. Half of my mom's siblings remained practicing Catholics; the other half fell away. In their adult years almost all my dad's siblings left their Lutheran faith. And in some ways, I don't blame the ones on both sides who left. As they were growing up, their faith communities were riddled with abuse and scandal; unfortunately, not much has changed. Nevertheless, growing up in a diverse family taught me so much, challenged me, and helped form me into who I am today.

My mom says that some people are born with a strong, vibrant spark of faith; she always believed that I was. She had many good reasons to believe this, and my own life as a kid is filled with examples. From a young age I was passionate about my faith life. Sometimes, even when only a few years old, I would give my parents a hard time if we didn't make it to Sunday Mass. My parents were faithful, but hardships during my childhood sometimes placed going to church on a lower priority, understandably so. Our lives had some very difficult moments, which I'll get into later. But even as a little kid I placed my faith first and I wanted to go to Mass as much as possible. Once I was old enough, if the rest of our family were going to miss Sunday Mass, I would often walk or ride my bike the mile to our parish. My mom believed I was born with passion for my faith.

I wasn't flashy about it, but from an early age I felt convicted to live out my faith and beliefs. When I was four or five years old, I set up lemonade stands to raise money for our local pregnancy help center. I didn't understand what these centers did, but in childlike simplicity and innocence I knew that those centers helped mothers and babies and that they needed support and that the work they did really mattered. And I wanted to help too.

My foundation of faith was always strong, but even stronger and more important was that my parents raised my siblings and me to have a deep respect and love for our fellow human beings. Whether it was our neighbors, other kids at school, children in hospitals, those experiencing homelessness, anyone who was struggling or suffering, we were taught to love everyone. We learned that how we treated others, how we interacted with them, reflected what we stood for and what we believed. I am still convicted of the deep value of each and every person and with the hatred, crime, racism, and civil unrest that pervades our world today it's heartbreaking to see that others have not been raised that same way. My parents raised us to love each person we met and to honor the dignity that each person deserves. My mom and dad grew up in homes riddled with abuse and neglect. Throughout their childhoods they struggled. Perhaps that's the source of their empathy (and, in turn, their children's). Remarkably, what happened to them as children did not destroy their openness and concern for others. Every day they worked to become better people, and they raised us to do the same.

My parents also raised us to respect every living being—animals too. We always had pets and my siblings and I still have a soft spot for them, especially rescue animals. We raised Leader Dogs for the Blind and throughout the years rescued dogs, frogs, birds, rats, hamsters, quail—all kinds of critters. My mom, an incredible gardener, taught us to respect the earth. We always had a vibrant garden and often took it upon ourselves to clean up trash throughout our local communities. We volunteered at senior living facilities, food banks and homeless shelters. My parents were truly "pro-life"—they lived it and they taught us to do the same. To us, "pro-life" always meant an all- encompassing life-affirming ethos. In the polarized political climate of the twenty-first century, the term has become controversial and disputed, but growing up we lived out "pro-life" in a way that was fully embodied, active. and positive. And I wish we saw more of that today.

I don't recall when my parents began to care about life issues, but one major event solidified our family's commitment. At the very beginning of my life, while still in utero, I had a twin sister. But a couple of months into the pregnancy my mom miscarried my twin and there was a point where it was touch-and-go with me as well. Thankfully, and obviously, I survived. While I was a little girl I heard my mom talk often about my twin and I remember thinking about her as a little angel looking down on me. Somewhere as a child I decided that she needed a name, so I've always called her "Cecilia." My youngest sister, Delia, looks astoundingly like me, so my family has also joked that Delia is the "twin that came back to haunt me."

Just as my mom has continued to carry the weight of that miscarriage, I have always carried my twin with me. My mom tells how the doctor told her and my dad that one of the babies no longer had a heartbeat; they hoped the baby would miscarry naturally, but neither they nor the doctors were sure what that would mean for me. Upon learning of the situation my mom's mother, my own grandmother, told her to throw herself down the stairs so the remaining living baby would miscarry and she could "try again." I can't imagine losing a child, but even more so I can't imagine being told (again, by your own mother, the child's grandmother!) to self-induce what essentially would be an abortion and to "try again." Perhaps, in part, that reflected the times. You don't know what you don't know, and I try not to hold that against my grandmother. Today so much more is known about pregnancy, fetal development, medicine, and miscarriage; today, perhaps, an exchange like the one between my mother and grandmother would never happen. Still, that story hurts my heart. Thankfully, my twin miscarried naturally and months later my mom gave birth to a hearty ten-pound fourteen-ounce baby—me.

My parents would suffer numerous other miscarriages—little lives that never got to flourish—but it seemed that my twin's death was the catalyst for their passionate respect for human life. My twin's short life led them to raise us to have steadfast respect for every human life, preborn or born. And other experiences throughout our lives also instilled our beliefs and our faith even more deeply.

When I was four years old, on his thirty-third birthday—the same age as Jesus when he died—my dad suffered a life-altering traumatic brain injury. To be completely honest, there was a time when we thought that my dad might not survive. He did survive, thank God, but ever since has suffered health setbacks and ailments. Most people would never notice my dad's chronic health issues because as a family we worked hard to take care of him, to make sure that he got rest and remained as vital as possible.

That same year my youngest sister and I were diagnosed with an extremely rare immune deficiency called Job Syndrome, named after the Old Testament figure who suffered greatly. Like Job, people with this syndrome suffer in many incomprehensible ways. Delia and I have suffered and we still do, often in silence because we are adamant about never drawing attention to our sickness. Only our parents and siblings know what we went through; only they witnessed the pain and suffering through most of our childhood. My sister and I never wanted Job Syndrome to define who we were, so we always tried to be strong and hide our ailments. But our hardships and struggles formed us into the resilient, empowered women we are today.

Job Syndrome—in medical terms, Hyper-IgE syndrome (HIES)—is an incredibly rare immune deficiency that can manifest itself in many ways, including regular illnesses (colds, flu, etc.), skin conditions (eczema, dermatitis, etc.), and respiratory issues (lung infections, pneumonia, etc.). My sister and I were among the first twenty-five documented cases in the US.; today there are only 250 throughout the world. I was four years old and Delia was a baby when we were diagnosed. Our parents were told to expect we would be hospitalized six to eight times a year, that we'd spend most of our childhood sick, and would "suffer greatly." Thankfully, our mother—a woman before her time—refused to let us suffer. Long before internet searches were common, before Whole Foods and plentiful organic food sections were readily available, she began researching vitamins, food allergies, and remedies that might help us. To this day my mom says that what empowered her, what encouraged her to ask questions and expect better for her children was La Leche League, an organization that empowers and helps mothers breastfeed their children and builds community around parents and their kids. My mom asked questions, tried anything and everything that could help, and found so much that worked for us. Instead of constantly being sick, we lived more or less normal lives. My experience with Job Syndrome was quite different from my sister's. Delia contracted frequent internal infections and regularly had pneumonia, whereas I grew up with terribly painful exterior elements, particularly extreme eczema.

Even when I was a few months old my baby pictures document my raw skin. Throughout my first few years things my mom tried helped a great deal, but my childhood eczema was so horrific that I often had open sores on the bottoms of my feet and lesions on my arms, legs, feet, and face. Even as an adult I still get bad bouts of it, but overall I have it pretty much under control.

My eczema emerged when I was an infant and got worse as I got older. By the time I was two or three, sometimes I would itch my scalp so hard that most of my hair would fall out; people often thought I had cancer and was going through chemotherapy. Once I was school age, my mom would bring me home at lunchtime every day to dampen my clothes, peel them off, and change them so what I was wearing wouldn't get stuck to my skin. After lunch she would take me back to school, then do the same thing before I went to bed at night.

In first grade my little face was red, and whenever I spoke up in class, I was bullied, mocked, and harassed. I wanted to be invisible. To take the attention off me and stop the harassment I quit speaking in class altogether. Prior to that I had been a strong, opinionated little girl who believed that she could accomplish anything she put her mind to. My parents would often joke that I was either going to be the "CEO of a Fortune 500 company or the dictator of a small nation," because I was so determined and passionate, and I would often direct my siblings. But as I started school I withered into a quiet, meek child with only one goal: never to draw attention to herself. Inside I was still the fierce and sassy girl I was born to be, but outside I had become the opposite.

Thankfully, as this began to unfold my parents recognized that something was wrong. When they figured out what was happening, they decided that I needed a "magic feather," something that would bring back the courageous little fighter that they knew and loved. They weren't going to let the bullies break me and I didn't want to let the bullies break me. They enrolled me in Irish dancing, and it changed my life. *Riverdance* had not yet come on the scene so only a few knew about Irish dancing, but it was unique, and I loved sharing this part of me, my heritage, and my culture with others. I still do. Irish dancing brought back my courage and spunk. It brought me back to life.

As I came back into my own, our family faced another hurdle. My brother, a year older, has always been one of my best friends and my constant "partner in crime." In fourth grade, Peter was diagnosed as being on the spectrum with autism. He was always the smartest person I knew, and still is. He probably was too smart for grade school, to be honest. Being like Doogie Howser, MD presents its own challenges. But Peter is now a PhD and a professor, so being incredibly intelligent also has its advantages. Peter's diagnosis, even though it was rare back then, opened opportunities for him and got him more support. It was a challenge for him and for my family but was another instance when our struggles brought us closer. My siblings—Peter, Moira, and Delia —are still close and I feel like we always will be, maybe because our struggles bonded us so closely. Through the years we became the four amigos, supporting—and challenging—each other, fighting through life's struggles together. My siblings and my parents are a gift, a consistent force for support, comfort, and love.

Throughout each chapter of my life, as I went through health, personal, and family struggles, my constant faith became even more critical and vibrant. In middle school I counted down the days until I could join the high school youth group. Then I could become more active in the church and have more opportunities to volunteer throughout the community. In high school, I jumped full throttle into my faith life: going to every youth group meeting, volunteering for every cause, going on mission trips, and organizing diocesan and community events. I felt a new freedom and a passion to make a difference. Around this time, I also became more engaged in issues concerning life and morality. I wanted to learn, to understand differing viewpoints, and to be challenged. With anyone who was willing I'd listen, offer my own perspective, or debate if they wanted to.

Abortion has always been personal to me, mainly because of my twin's death and, frankly, how close I myself came to not being born. Some might dismiss my experience, but even from a very young age I felt like a survivor. I had overcome so much. I recognized my own fragility and was always happy just to be alive, even when I was really suffering. I try to emulate that in my life today. Only in my early teens did I hear the full story about my twin and my own grandmother encouraging a forced miscarriage so my mother could «try again." My parents felt it was appropriate to tell me only then, but they believed that I deserved to know. And once I knew that story, abortion became even more intensely personal for me. One way or another, abortion seems to have impacted almost everyone I know.

As I grew older, I seized every opportunity to speak up for women and their children. I've always respected other people's lives, experiences, and perspectives, but my particular form of teenage rebellion was to wear t-shirts with life-affirming messages, even though many of my high school peers proclaimed that they were pro-choice. I found wearing them at school, events, parties, even family gatherings, to be edgy and interesting. At street fairs one of my favorite pastimes was walking up to booths that were promoting abortion, asking questions, and sparking discussions. I was never aggressive, just inquisitive. I've always believed that many things in the world would be different if we just listened to each other's perspective, asked questions, and shared our own life experiences and perspectives. I looked for every opportunity to engage in discussions and debates, but always with love. I was always ready to share my beliefs and perspectives on faith, chastity, the world, anything else anyone wanted to discuss. And the best part is that my views and understanding of various topics and issues evolved in beautiful ways. And I'm still evolving. Growing up, I encountered some things I never would have considered to be "life issues." But over the years I've become passionate about any topic that has human dignity at its heart—immigration, education, health, and so much more. I struggle these days to know where I fit in the "pro-life" world, or if the term "pro-life" as many understand it represents my stance. I'm passionate about being consistent and I recognize the importance of numerous "life" issues. I'm passionate about women's health and through my own experiences (including those of friends and many others I've met throughout the years) I am convinced that women should always feel like they have other options *besides* abortion. We need to do better in providing support to all women in their lives, careers, and familial situations. My passion about dignity and respect for all human life will always be paramount.

A certain incident during my teenage years opened my eyes to the fragility of life and made me realize that "pro-life"—at least to me—means way more than opposition to abortion. When I was fifteen my grandfather committed suicide. I remember that day vividly. Every Sunday I worked in the church nursery, babysitting for parents who wanted to go to Mass without screaming kids and shenanigans. Every morning my grandfather's twin sister would call him, but that morning he didn't pick up the phone, so she was worried. She called my dad, who decided to drop me off at the church then drive the fifteen minutes to my grandfather's house to make sure everything was OK. Even today, I remember the moment my dad dropped me off. I knew that something was wrong, that something had happened. But I could never have imagined how our lives were about to change, nor could I ever have imagined what did happen.

When my mom picked me up a few hours later, she told me that my grandfather had taken his own life. He had recently been diagnosed with Parkinson's disease and one of his flaws (and he had many) was his need to control. He was obsessed not only with controlling others' lives, but also his own. His sense that he was about to lose control over his life made him end it.

In that moment my eyes opened to a fuller understanding of what "pro-life" means. It's about the entirety of human life—preborn children, the elderly, the suffering, the homeless, those who are lonely, those who are forgotten, refugees, every single person.

Experiences and exchanges that filled my teen-age years challenged me in new ways and fueled my fire to become more active on all issues related to the dignity of human life. I had nearly lost my own life in utero, nearly lost my dad to a head injury, lost my grandfather to suicide. During my teenage years my eyes began to be opened to the need to be consistent in valuing and protecting every human life.

My early life laid a foundation for many things that have been built upon it. In hindsight, it's almost as if each was a stone, and piece by piece my life grew into the strong, stable structure it is today. And that structure has always been sheltered beneath a stead-fast roof—my faith— especially during the difficult moments. When I was bullied and taunted my faith showed me how to regain my direction and gave me the strength and grace to understand my aggressors and have compassion for them. When my faith or beliefs were challenged I never wandered from what I knew to be intrinsic and true. When I was attacked for what I believed, I always attempted to find com-mon ground and to understand the other person's perspective. When your structure is strong, you won't crumble when adversity comes.

My early life turned me into a seeker. Though I was clear and strong about my own beliefs, I wanted to understand the paths that other people were fol-lowing; I was open to their perspectives. Every time someone excluded me because of my eczema or for other surface-level reasons, I worked even harder to understand where they were coming from. Every person that attacked my faith and beliefs inspired me to understand their perspective and simultaneously made my faith and beliefs stronger. I know this is not everyone's experience, but this was mine. My grandfather's suicide made me respect all human life and find even deeper compassion for those who were suffering. From the preborn to the elderly, I have always wanted to be a voice for those who have no voice, to promote the value of every human person.

One of the greatest gifts of faith, in my experience, is the beauty and power that it instills and unlocks. It doesn't matter what you believe or whether you practice any kind of religion. Just making the space to quiet your mind and to connect with yourself and the world, reminding yourself of who you are and who you were created to be--that can be powerful. You are royalty. You are the child of a King. You were made for greatness. But sometimes we need to make space in our lives to remind ourselves of that. My faith has quieted the voices inside my head that tell me that I don't matter, that my voice doesn't matter, even that my life doesn't matter. We were created for a unique purpose, a mission in this world— and we were created in love, for love, to be loved. If above all else each of us endeavored to love, our world would be transformed.

Chapter 2

University Life

How Living Faithfully in the Real World Transformed My Life and My Faith

As high school drew to a close, like so many other teenagers trying to figure things out, I had not yet formed an idea of what I wanted to be, where I wanted to go next, or what my future held. Before heading off to college, I decided to take a year off to figure my life out, and during that year I wanted to give back. I had already been through so much in my young life and felt so blessed, that I wanted to devote time to helping others. My parents always instilled that no matter how difficult life was or whatever darkness we had gone through or were going through, we should look for the glimmers of hope and the blessings. All my life I've been criticized for being too positive—about myself or others—but I've always found that when you look outside yourself and your own struggles you find new opportunities for hope and unexpected blessings. I know that life can be hard and painful, but I remind myself every day that, no matter what, God is good and is always working in our lives. And everyone's life is a journey. Even for those who may be non-spiritual or non-religious, goodness (and good things!) will always reign. Everything we go through, good and bad, leads us to becoming the person we are meant to be and to discovering where we're supposed to be. Sometimes the difficult things we go through teach us how to help and to empower others. At age eighteen, I decided to get out of my own bubble and help others. That decision changed my life.

Throughout high school, I had regularly volunteered with my youth group at St. Leo's Soup Kitchen in Detroit. I really connected with the space, the workers, and the people being served there. At the end of my shift I enjoyed grabbing a tray and finding an open chair among the hundreds of guests who came there every day. I would try to sit with a new person every time, but I also got to know the regulars and would often catch up with them too. I always felt a deep connection to that soup kitchen, perhaps because my maternal grandfather, to whom I was close, went to St. Leo's school and being there provided a connection to him. I always felt at home there. So that was the first thing I did during my "sabbatical" year.

A few times a week I drove to downtown Detroit in my little Ford Focus, which my uncle affectionately nicknamed "The Chastinator" because the back was covered with bumper stickers about life, human dignity, and chastity. That car was always a good conversation starter, especially when a random person would ask about one or another of the stickers. My parents worried about The Chastinator getting keyed or vandalized and about my personal safety, but nothing like that ever happened. Perhaps it would be a different story now, but at that time most people respected me, and my car.

While volunteering at St. Leo's and at a local pregnancy help center, I also held a part-time job. My parents supported my decision to spend my time like that while I figured out what I wanted to do for college and in life, but they worried about my finances. They never graduated from college yet are the smartest people I know. Growing up we always had enough money but struggling through numerous economic recessions taught us to be frugal. When people bring up "the recession," my mom always says facetiously, "which one?" Because they had grown up with so little, they spent as little as possible yet were very generous with others and taught us to be the same way. Frugality does not mean stinginess; my parents are the most generous people I know. Their mindset is to conserve your money wisely so you never owe more than you can handle and never put yourself in a difficult financial position that you can't dig yourself out of. Even though at times we did struggle financially, they worked for everything they had and provided a harmonious life for us. My parents would prioritize our needs and make things happen that we wanted, like Irish dance lessons or Catholic school for my freshman year of high school. They would've loved to pay for our college, but we did it on our own. I was always a good saver, so I knew I could handle postponing college and my career for a year.

Looking back, even though college and graduate school have definitely opened opportunities for me, I would've been fine if I hadn't gone. I have always been driven and I was always chasing dreams and passions, so while my life may have taken a different path had I not pursued higher education, I don't think college is necessary to be successful. My parents never pressured me about what I was going to do in life; rather, they encouraged me and my siblings to be open to where life would take us. They never pressured us regarding "vocation" either, although in high school and even more so in college I experienced pressure from others to "choose my vocation"—find someone and get married or join a convent—and "figure it out." That's a story that I'll get back to later, but I spent my teenage years trying to figure out who I was and the person that I am still becoming.

I can't explain how certain things in my life worked out, especially the times when I volunteered instead of working for a salary, yet somehow I made enough money to pay my bills and afford college tuition. I do know that God blesses our faithfulness. And that's something I need to remind myself every day, especially now, when I think back on everything I've done and everything I've overcome. God is always faithful, always walking with us, and always there— even when we don't feel God's presence. And even when we dismiss, ignore, even get frustrated with or angry at God, God is always there, waiting for us, loving us. Whenever I felt God calling me to something, no matter how difficult or crazy, blessings would pour out and any question or issue I was facing was solved. So, although my parents were concerned about my future, when I took a year off God provided whatever I needed to follow the path that lay before me.

That gap year was transformative. I learned about myself, met many interesting people, experienced new things, and came to understand so much more about the world. I would encourage any young person to think about taking time off, be it before college or after, or a "sabbatical" at some point during your career. We get so busy—my life is a perfect example—that we don't take time to recognize the beautiful things happening around us. Even right now, sitting here stressing about all the things I need to get done today, I remind myself to take a breath, breathe in and out, enjoy the sunshine, spend time with friends, find ways to feed my heart and soul, and then to do those things. That gap year was my first experience of taking a "life breath." We need to pull ourselves out of our everyday bubble and be open, learn from others, be challenged—and take time to breathe.

After that year, even though after volunteering and working only part-time I had little in my bank account, I did decide to go to college. And God opened doors and poured out the blessings. I chose Ave Maria College in Ypsilanti, Michigan, a small school not far from my family. It had a great liberal arts program that would give me options and provide opportunities for the future. I got a scholarship and some financial support, and miraculously was able to make up the rest through the generosity of others and by picking up part-time work where I could. The summer after my first year, I decided to embrace another adventure, which many thought was crazy. I knew that I needed to jump at the opportunity, and I felt confident that the money would take care of itself.

When I was thirteen I had read about the "Crossroads Pro-Life Walk Across America," and ever since had wanted to join the college-aged young people taking an entire summer to walk 3,000 miles, from the West Coast to the East Coast. My parents told me I could do it when I turned eighteen, probably hoping that I would lose interest or forget about it. But I didn't. They have always supported whatever crazy idea or dream I've come up with, but Crossroads made them worry about my safety and well-being. As you can imagine, walking across America, no matter how cautious and careful you are, can be dangerous. You never know what or who you might encounter. Unfortunately, pedestrians are hit by cars every day and walking through unfamiliar places, as we would be doing, would make such accidents even more likely. And this was before smartphones and social media, making things even more complicated. But I was determined to do the walk and sure enough, I did.

During my freshman year at Ave Maria, someone from Crossroads came to speak. Afterwards, I could think about nothing else for the coming summer.

That same year I also got connected with Stand True Ministries, an organization that travelled to music festivals to talk to festival goers about faith, life, relationships, whatever people had on their hearts and minds. I didn't realize then how these two organizations and these two opportunities would change my life. My experience at Ave Maria was great, but my energy always has been (and probably always will be) dedicated not to academics but to making a difference in the world. I embraced college life, took some great classes, and got to know incredible people. Many are dear friends that I still have today. But my main focus really was on the summer. I could hardly wait for classes to conclude and for my adventure across America to begin. I had no idea what I was in for, nor that I would face adversity and would have a rocky start. But that summer turned out to be life-changing.

I had never been to California and was excited to experience the beauty of the Golden State. In May 2004 I flew there, planning to enjoy some sightseeing while spending a few days with Aunt Alice and her family in Berkeley. It would be good to relax with them before setting out on the three-month walk. On numerous things, including our views on politics and life issues, my aunt and I are polar opposites. She knew why I was coming to California but I hoped our differing views would not disrupt our relationship. Plus, I was only nineteen so she could write off our disagreements as naiveté or immaturity—or so I thought. As I boarded that flight to San Francisco, I never imagined what the next few days and months would bring.

After Aunt Alice picked me up at SFO I was excited to see James and Tom, my twelve- and sixteen-year-old cousins. For the first day or two we did not talk politics or religion or anything like that, but something did seem to be percolating. My visit was about to take a very sharp turn. I think Tom knew why I had come to California, but James kept peppering me with questions about why I was walking across the US. "Are you walking for cancer? My friend did a walk for diabetes, is that why you're walking?" The questions kept coming. He was trying to pinpoint my motives, and I don't blame him. But before I left I had promised my dad to not bring up anything controversial and to focus on having a "nice visit" with his sister. I had buried the t-shirts for the walk at the bottom of my suitcase and tried to enjoy a non-confrontational visit with family. I loved to talk about faith, politics, and issues that I cared about, but I've always recognized that there is a time and place for those discussions. This was not one of those times. But the questions kept coming and finally, sitting at a restaurant with Alice, Tom, and James, my younger cousin asked again. "Kate, but why are you walking across America?"

I looked to my aunt, hoping that she would redirect the conversation, but instead she doubled down. "Yes, Kate, why are you walking?" I don't know if she knew the agreement that I had made with my dad or if she was being edgy or was testing me to see what I would say, but Alice snarkily asked the question again, "Well, Kate, why are you walking?" I took a big gulp of water and a deep breath and said, "Well, I'm walking for all life and the respect of all people—old people, babies, people with disabilities, everyone." It was a way of explaining "pro-life" without mentioning the term abortion, or anything of the like. Just the simple and honest explanation that I was walking for the respect of all people and all life. James looked at me, then at his mom, and then in the most innocent way said, "Mom, I don't understand why anyone would *murder* a baby before they were born." Nothing I had said could have led James to say that. I didn't mention abortion or even use the term "pro-life," but my cousin must have been thinking about it or one of his friends had brought it up at school. So when I offered a "sugar-coated explanation" of the life issue, he connected the dots.

At that moment my aunt's head exploded and her eyes nearly popped out of her head, as did mine. She was so upset, I thought she might start tipping over tables. She muttered something I couldn't make out and ordered us to go get in the car. We started driving to my cousin's soccer practice in complete silence until the boys got out. On our drive back to the house, when it was just the two of us, Alice unleashed her fury. In many instances throughout my young life I had learned to react calmly to adverse situations. Looking back, all those moments had prepared me for this car ride. My aunt started yelling at me about George W. Bush, who was president at the time. I responded that this wasn't a political walk nor did it have anything to do with George W. Bush. To me, the life issue was never political—it is personal. And, as I've said before, to most people abortion is personal because abortion is pervasive. Almost everyone has a personal connection to or experience with that issue. She yelled at me about women's rights and how naive I was and how I didn't know what I was doing or talking about. Looking back, I definitely was naive —I was only nineteen. But I also knew what I was talking about and, even at nineteen, I had a depth of knowledge and understanding beyond that of many adults. I didn't get defensive, I just listened. I was raised to listen to others and to work to understand their points of view. So I did listen, then would offer my opinion if and when the right moment presented itself. I sought to understand where my aunt was coming from, but I also wasn't going to discard my own deeply held beliefs and experiences. My pro-life views were personal, just as I'm sure hers were. I recognized that, but I'm not sure that she did.

When we arrived at the house I exhaled deeply. "We made it," I thought. Maybe if I stayed out of her way we could get through the next few days without any more confrontation. Then I could go on my way and join the Crossroads team for our walk across America. But as we stepped into the house, Alice, in her frustration and anger, turned and yelled, "I'm going to work and I don't want you to be here when I get back." I stood in the hallway, stunned, as she stormed back out. On the one hand I understood her frustration and anger, but on the other I was a nineteen-year-old kid who had barely been away from home, much less to California. I burst into tears. I called my mom crying and she snapped into "mama bear" mode. I'm still surprised that she didn't fly out to California and lay the smackdown with Aunt Alice. My dad snapped into his military mode and came up with a plan. He knew the area from his time in the Navy and found a hotel, made a reservation, and sent a taxi—the first I had ever ridden in. Sobbing, I stuffed my belongings into my suitcase and hopped in for the ride to the hotel. I didn't find out until months later that, as cool and collected as my dad seemed, he was stressed. He had to go to Staples to fax a copy of his credit card to the hotel (this was before the times of paying online or over the phone). Taking my car to run his errand, he agitatedly shoved the rearview mirror and shattered the entire windshield. My family still laughs about how my dad is so powerful that he can break a windshield without incurring a single scratch. At the hotel that night I contacted Crossroads, and the next day they came to pick me up. It seemed I had been destined to start my adventure early.

My aunt and I remain cordial, but we have never again spoken about that day. I still can't fathom kicking anyone out of my house for their beliefs, especially not my brother's daughter, a nineteen-year-old kid away from home in an unfamiliar place. But I have compassion for Alice. This story represents so much of what people experience every day, especially if they have deeply held beliefs. My aunt was raised in a family that was plagued with abuse and pain, and like my mother and so many others, in her adult life she broke free from her shackles. Many women in her circles pursued a pathway to freedom via Betty Friedan's *Feminine Mystique* and the sexual revolution, but looking back I ask myself: was that truly freedom? I struggle with the idea that women can find freedom through abortion or sex. I have never comprehended how using someone else for your own sexual pleasure or, for that matter, using any human being for anything or killing a vulnerable human being would bring true liberation. Call me naive or whatever you want, but I've never been able to understand that. To me, the sexual revolution and the prevalence of abortion in our culture has not opened up opportunities for women or freed them from exploitation and objectification—in fact, it has amplified that trajectory.

My aunt's caustic reaction reveals that at some level she also feels the same inherent tension that I do when it comes to abortion and the sexual revolution, a tension that is difficult for many women to face--especially in a culture that can make life difficult for them. That experience with my aunt confirmed a path I had been on all my life, the path of a seeker set on encountering others and striving to understand their perspectives. I took this lesson to heart and ended up carrying it with me the entire summer with Crossroads. Every weekend we would reach a new major city and would speak at churches and community groups, do service projects, and encounter people on the streets from all backgrounds, beliefs, and walks of life. As we were walking we talked to people who saw our pro-life shirts and wanted to ask questions, debate us, or show their support or disagreement. We saw some lives saved and others lost. We encountered women who embraced abortion and others who felt they had no other choice because they were being "encouraged" or even coerced by a boyfriend or family member. I met many, many people that summer and each one had a different story. But I sought to listen and understand and show compassion to each one—just as I tried to do with my aunt. I've come to recognize that we never really know what someone else is going through. But even though we may never know what they're going through, we can listen to their stories with love and compassion. This is a lesson that I relive every day of my life—and I hope you will too. How different the world would look if we endeavored to understand every person we met with love and compassion.

After that summer, I carried my experiences back into college, asking more questions and looking for commonality and answers. I dedicated the next summer to Stand True Ministries, traveling around the US to music festivals, doing outreach by talking to people about faith, life, abortion, chastity, relationships, and anything else they wanted to talk about. Again, my parents were concerned about my finances but supported my decision. And again, God provided. During both my summer with Crossroads and the next with Stand True, many friends, family, even strangers stepped in to support me, and with student loans and scholarships I was able to pay my personal expenses and manage to have enough for school.

Stand True was another summer of conversations, challenges, and transformation. The group was predominantly Evangelical. Although I grew up in a mixed-faith family, I didn't have a lot of experience speaking with people from other religious backgrounds—especially Evangelicals who knew their faith. My dad came from a non-practicing Evangelical family, and my mom's was Catholic in name only. Throughout my life I've had friends from Evangelical, Jehovah's Witness, Mormon, Muslim, Sikh, atheist, and so many other backgrounds, but before college I never really talked to them about faith. With Stand True, for the first time in my life I encountered people of different faith backgrounds who knew what they believed, loved it, and wanted to talk about it. And I was the same—I knew my faith, loved it, and wanted to talk about it with anyone who was willing. For hours our group would debate theology as we drove across state lines to yet another festival, listening to music and bantering about life and pop culture. We really loved being together, listening to one another, having healthy discussions and debates. For the first time in my life I really felt seen and heard. Not everyone agreed with my point of view but they definitely respected it. On tour that summer I learned and grew. On that tour I would debate faith topics constantly with one guy who became one of my best friends. He ended up becoming an Evangelical pastor. That summer I learned about life, the world, and how to interact, even in small ways. with those I disagreed with. I encountered people who were steadfast in their beliefs, knew their faith and had a firm stance on everything, yet were always open and willing to discuss anything. That summer I had so much fun listening to live music and staying up until all hours, chit-chatting about life, faith, and whatever was on our minds.

We were passionate for our faith and steadfast in our beliefs. But even more steadfast was our love for each other and our fellow human beings. That summer, I learned to look at all people that I disagreed with, whether in or out of the faith community, as my brothers and sisters. Above all else I was called to love them. We're all called to love.

Besides my conversations with this crew and what I learned from them, that summer transformed me in many other ways. That summer I decided to recommit to chastity as an adult because I had evolved away from *I Kissed Dating Goodbye* to understanding chastity as the perfection of love; that summer, right before my eyes, I witnessed a baby's life saved.

Ever since I was fifteen, when I had asked my mom for a "True Love Waits" chastity ring, I had kept it on my finger. As I got into college, however, I wanted a more "adult" symbol. In high school True Love Waits was trendy, but I wanted something that more fully embodied my commitment. I wanted something subtle yet meaningful. At one of the music festivals I found a ring inscribed with "John 3:16" in Greek. It was perfect—it was subtle and could mean a lot of things, but it also embodied God's love and commitment to us. In the same way, I wanted a ring that would embody my love and commitment to a future husband. I'm not yet married, so I still wear this ring, and still stand by my commitment—and I strive to live out this commitment every day.

A second transformative experience that summer was the story of "Baby B." One day while I was managing the booth at a festival in nowhere, Illinois, a young guy with a mohawk walked up and started talking to me. I remember thinking how cool this guy—let's call him Johnny—seemed. At one point he glanced at the table and started flipping through one of the books we had there. I kept bantering about who knows what when all of a sudden he raised his face, his eyes filled with tears. Thinking that something I had said upset him, I started to apologize. But he quickly said "No, no, it's not that," and went on to say how earlier that day his girlfriend had called to tell him that she was pregnant and had scheduled an abortion. Externally I was calm and collected, but internally I was freaking out. I didn't know how to help or what to say, so I prayed, asking God to give me the words. A friend in high school would often say: "God doesn't call the qualified, he qualifies the called." Maybe this was one of those instances? At least I hoped it was. Because I had no idea what to say or do. As I stood there in the big event tent, my mind was percolating, I asked Johnny if he wanted to go somewhere quieter to talk. He said, "Yes."

We walked outside and sat at a table, where we talked and talked. For hours. We talked about life, relationships, family, struggles, joy, and much more. We had never met before, but it felt like we had known each other for years. We talked about his girlfriend and his preborn child, and how he wanted to keep the baby but didn't feel like he had a choice because it's a "woman's issue." I listened to everything he was saying, encouraging him simply to be present to his girlfriend (and in turn, present for their child). Sometimes we don't know what words to say—at that moment I definitely didn't—and with regards to his girlfriend Johnny didn't either. But sometimes being present is enough. After the two of us sat at that picnic table talking, for hours, we made a plan. He would reach out to her, talk to her, and reaffirm that he was there for her, that whatever she decided they were in this together. I gave him my cell number, and he walked away. I didn't know if I would ever hear from him or ever see him again, so all I could do was pray. And oh, did I pray. And I had everyone I knew praying. Above all, I hoped that Johnny and his girlfriend felt supported and loved.

A couple of days later, as we were packing up to drive to the next festival, I was about to hop into the van when I heard someone yell "Kate! Hey, Kate . . . wait!" I turned around—It was Johnny. I was surprised to see him again, and so quickly. He asked if I had a few minutes to talk because he had something that he wanted to share. I wasn't sure what he was going to say, but I said "Yes." Johnny told me that after we talked, he had taken all the information I had given him (I had no idea which brochures he took) and spent the entire festival reading through them over and over again. He took my advice and called his girlfriend to let her know that she wasn't alone, and that whatever she decided, he would stand with her. As he was talking, I was on the edge of my seat. . . Everything we had talked about, everything he had shared was flooding through my mind. And then, finally, Johnny said that they had a really good conversation. They laughed, they cried, and they ended up deciding to keep their baby! This year "Baby B," as I like to call him, turns sixteen. Wow. This story still blows my mind when I think about it.

I learned many lessons those two summers, but the greatest is to listen, to be open, and—above all—be present. There is incredible power in simply being present and listening. The world would look so different if we did just those two things.

Chapter 3

How College Informed My Faith and Beliefs

A ve Maria College and Franciscan University of Steubenville differ from state and secular schools, and not in the ways you would expect. Both identify themselves as authentically Catholic and both uphold the teachings of the Roman Catholic Church. Some think that Catholic colleges and universities like these indoctrinate their students, oppress them, and stifle their freedom to think for themselves. In reality, both schools taught me to think independently, ask questions, challenge my professors, and evaluate what I was learning. They also taught me to examine everything I was taught or told as well as the world's status quo. My education at Ave Maria and Franciscan was paramount in my journey to adulthood and set me up for success in my career and my life. The greatest gift of all, though, was that my education taught me to think.

Because both schools were small, I had opportunities that a large university could not provide. I knew most students, at least by face and name, and got to know many others in a deeper way. I knew about their lives and their families and formed some of my deepest friendships during those college years. My classes and professors challenged me and unleashed a freedom of knowledge that I never knew existed. My professors at Franciscan regularly encouraged us to do our own research, to challenge what they were teaching, and to draw our own conclusions—especially if we could back up our reasoning with evidence and defend our position. On their exams, professors encouraged us to bring up new ideas and arguments and rewarded our courage and tenacity. From what friends and others tell me about their education, this is rare in the academic world and I am grateful for what I experienced. Ave Maria and Franciscan led me further on my journey as a "seeker" and taught me to be open to other perspectives; I discovered how to always be searching and learning, never letting my self-induced isolation or stubbornness hold me back from the opportunity to be enlightened or challenged.

College also made me understand success in a new way. Although my dad did take a couple of college classes throughout his career, my parents didn't have academic degrees. But they were successful; they're two of the best-informed people I know. Sit with them for an episode of Jeopardy and you will see what I mean—they know everything. Some of my peers wanted to get into medicine or finance or some other career where they would earn a lot of money, but my parents' example taught me that making a huge salary doesn't guarantee a happy, successful, full life. I learned to keep my priorities straight, put God and family first, and rely on divine providence for what I need--even though it might not come in the way that I expect. Many situations throughout my life—like my "gap year" and the summers I volunteered with Crossroads and Stand True—showed me how God always provides. But only in college did I begin to understand the depth and power of God's providence.

More than ever the many definitions of success are a topic of constant discussion. To some success means money; others look to the number of followers on social media; others define it as freedom and flexibility. Life and business coaching has become a massive market—especially for women. People crave fame and fortune, but at the heart of it all we want to be known and loved. And that happens when we're in our right place, living out the life that we were created for—not chasing whatever version of "success" the world tells us to pursue. One of the first books that I read in college, Viktor Frankl's *Man's Search for Meaning*, changed my life. Frankl opened my eyes in numerous ways, but above all he instilled a beautiful perspective on the definition of success. In this small book, jam-packed with invaluable life lessons, Frankl writes of success:

> Don't aim at success. The more you aim at it and make it a target, the more you are going to miss it. For success, like happiness, cannot be pursued; it must ensue, and it only does so as the unintended side effect of one's personal

dedication to a cause greater than oneself or as the by-product of one's surrender to a person other than oneself. Happiness must happen, and the same holds for success: you have to let it happen by not caring about it. I want you to listen to what your conscience commands you to do and go on to carry it out to the best of your knowledge. Then you will live to see that in the long-run—in the long-run, I say!—success will follow you precisely because you had forgotten to think about it. (Beacon Press [1992], 12)

Reading Frankl was another "suddenly" moment for me. I had been raised with and was continuing to live out an understanding of success like his—including which school(s) I chose and how I dealt with my college career—but never had anyone encapsulated it for me in this way. I had never been taught to chase money, college scholarships, or a career. I was taught to be authentic, to be the person I was created to be. The world would look different if each person chose as a life goal to be the person he or she has been created to be. We each need to figure out who we were created to be, and I'm beginning to realize that this work may take a lifetime; every single day I'm still *becoming* more of who I was created to be. We are as unique as our fingerprints. If we believed in our uniqueness and adopted Frankl's definition of success, our lives and our world would look very different—in a really good way. I loved Frankl's book and still do. I try to re-read it every few years and probably should do so more often.

Man's Search for Meaning was foundational to my formation in college, but many other puzzle pieces of my academic story compose the picture of what was to come in my life. Because I loved my faith and was interested in learning more, I chose to study theology. Family members and others would sometimes say snarky things like, "Are you studying to be a nun?" or "Are you going to be the first female pope?" It took everything in me not to roll my eyes at comments like that. They didn't understand my decision to study something simply because it interested me nor did they understand why I was willing to go into debt for something that I may never use in a career or that might not lead to what the world views as "success." Earning my degree from Franciscan proved to be one of the best decisions I ever made, and the best foundation for what was to come.

The thoughtful, respectful professors there listened to students' arguments about faith, biblical principles, theology, life, and anything else we wanted to discuss. They encouraged us to challenge what they said, what we read, and what we were learning, and to do our own research and come to our own conclusions. This attitude, so rare especially in today's academic world, is one of the many reasons why going into debt for a theology degree from an orthodox Catholic university was one of the best investments I've yet made. Although I've never taught theology or done anything specifically in the realm of that discipline, since my graduation not a day has gone by that I haven't used what I learned at Ave Maria and Franciscan.

In the Fall of 2005, after my first semester at Steubenville, I signed up to study abroad. I'm sure my parents were thinking that it would have been better for me to stay the course in Ohio and not take out more student loans to study abroad, but I decided to go for it and they were incredibly supportive. And once again, somehow my finances and everything else fell into place, allowing me to embark on another transformative chapter of my life.

During that semester abroad, I would stand in the front row at St. Peter's Square to see Pope Benedict XVI (I still have that picture!), travel to Ireland for the first time (now it's my second home), travel through Austria, Belgium, Bosnia, Croatia, France, Germany, Italy, Poland, and other countries, sleep in train stations, almost get pickpocketed, walk through a minefield without getting blown up (if you know, you know). I could tell many stories, but one prominent experience related to that semester occurred even before I left the US.

A few weeks before flying to Austria, my first time out of the US (besides Canada, but that doesn't count for Michiganders because we're so close to the border), my mom's family held its annual Christmas party. Some relatives are amazingly supportive and loving toward me, but throughout the years I've also faced a great deal of adversity. At family events it can feel like I have a target on my back. From a young age I learned to be on guard and not share too much personal information because you never know what can and will be used against you. I learned not to take these attacks personally, as they most likely reflected unresolved issues from before I was born. Every family has them. But I've learned to live with it and try to dodge the bullets. Just before this Christmas party I had turned twenty-one and was excited to join my older cousins and family members and finally drink a beer. I was looking forward to catching up with everyone and sharing the big news that in a few weeks I would be heading overseas. Overall, my family was very supportive. Some gave me a few dollars to have a pint on them, others handed me prayer intentions to take with me to the holy pilgrimage sites I would be visiting, but Aunt Patricia spent most of the party ignoring me.

After a while, though, every time she walked past she began to make random comments about my ring, the one with John 3:16 etched in Greek: "For God so loved the world, He gave His only son." The ring could've represented a lot of things. For a few years I had been wearing it on my right hand as a reminder of God's love for me and my love for and commitment to my future husband. People rarely commented and not a single person in the family had ever asked me about it. I have always been happy to explain the meaning and why I wear it, but I never really promoted it because, honestly, it's not really anyone else's business. And on the other hand, I've never made a huge splash about it because it's a normal part of my life. People assumed it was decorative or meant something to me—which it does. I never brought it up and never made a big deal about it. To be completely honest, her comments seemed bizarre. What was going on puzzled me.

Most family members know—or they think they know—only what I've told them about my stand on issues of faith, chastity, and life. We usually didn't talk much about the topics that we disagree on, but every so often someone would come in with a BANG and start a discussion or debate. From a very young age, I had a policy (You might be thinking, what little kid has a policy? But I had to.) that I wouldn't bring anything up myself, but if someone raised a topic that I cared about I could not be silent. Throughout the years Patricia, who never bothered to ask me why I was committed to chastity or what my ring stood for, had made many assumptions about who I am and what I believe. And she wasn't the only one. Many family members, friends, and even strangers make assertions about my life and beliefs, a pattern that continues today.

So, at this Christmas party, I'm walking around with my baby cousin Kaitlin on my hip, and Patricia kept walking by and making comments about my ring. At one point, she grabbed my hand and snarkily said, "Oh, are you married now?" I pulled my hand away and kept walking. I had become indifferent to such harassment at family functions. I wasn't going to let somebody else's insecurities or personal issues affect me. So I ignored her commentary and focused on having fun, but she was nearly incessant. "What's with the ring? Most people don't wear rings like that until they're married, are you married?" I kept a straight face and continued trying to ignore her. But then, even though I had little Kaitlin in my arms, as she was leaving Patricia came to give me a hug and said, "I want you to take advantage of being abroad. Let go of this 'chastity thing' and just have sex. . . Have sex with someone from every country and anyone else you want. No one will know. No one will ever know!" Meanwhile, numerous family members were standing around or walking through the dining area where we were talking. Mortified and embarrassed, at first I just stood there—in shock. She continued, "You need to stop with your sex hang-ups. How do you know until you've had some? You can't possibly know what you want until you've had some!"

Wow. You can imagine how awkward this was, standing in a room full of people, many of them over-hearing her commentary but saying nothing. Perhaps they were all in shock, too. Here I was, just turned twenty-one, joyfully walking around the party with my little cousin, excited about the Austrian adventure I was about to go on. Then Patricia launched her words into the air. After I shook off the shock, I found the courage to respond, but not in a defensive way. I knew that being defensive wouldn't be helpful and wouldn't get me anywhere, so I decided to be flippant and go back to a comment she made to me years before. Learning that I was going to study theology this same aunt said, "You're studying theology. Are you going to become a nun?" Standing in that dining room, a baby on my hip, I turned to my aunt and said facetiously, "Oh, I don't need to do that. I'm going to become a nun. I'm actually going over to Europe to look at convents." I thought this comment might nip her sarcasm and get her to leave me alone, but it only fired her up even more.

"How could you do something like that when you don't even know what you're missing?" she asked. I remained calm and collected, making random comments, spouting anything I could think of in hopes that it might defuse the tension. In all honesty, some things were dumb but I hoped that anything I said or did, perhaps something that seemed immature, might get her off my case. I remember blurting out, "Boys are dumb, throw rocks at them." Which is hysterical, looking back at it. I was definitely too old to be saying something like that, but I was tossing out anything I could think of. Anything to get her to leave me alone.

Throughout my entire life I have dealt with baseless, personal attacks, so I have learned not to take the bait and not to take these things personally. Back in my early days people would make cruel comments about how I looked or about my eczema, so this was nothing new but my aunt continued stoking the fire, tossing condescending comments at me. Meanwhile my mother, sitting at the table with a few other family members, heard what was going on. Mom stood up and yelled at Patricia, "It must be worth something if they all want it!" So simple, yet so true. We had grown up hearing those words because it struck a chord when a childhood friend of my mom's in Detroit once said that to her. Somewhere amid my commentary, my aunt's responses, and my mom yelling those words, Patricia finally gave up and headed home.

To give this incident more context, when I was a little kid this same aunt called Child Protective Services on my parents because of my terrible eczema. We had gone time and time again to the University of Michigan for testing and resources, but they couldn't figure out how to help me. My mom figured out how to treat my eczema and ailments by herself. Yet Aunt Patricia took it upon herself to call CPS, claiming that my parents were "withholding medical treatment." Which was totally false. It's repulsive to think that someone—a relative—would call CPS on the best parents four little kids could ever have and how that one call could have affected our entire lives. It even could have caused the authorities to remove us from our home. I don't tell this part of my story to throw Patricia under the bus, but if I'm going to take advice—sexual or otherwise—from anyone, it wouldn't be from the person who could've caused me to be taken away from my amazing parents. I've forgiven her, but what I share here is important to understanding my next comment.

If someone attacks you for your beliefs, especially when they've not even taken the time to get to know you or tried to understand why you believe what you believe, their concerns usually reflect more about them than anything about you. I don't know exactly what my aunt was thinking or why she came after me that day (or any other time that she's come after me), but my perception is that I make her uncomfortable because I've lived life differently than she and the rest of her family and friends have. I want to give her the benefit of the doubt to think that she was genuinely concerned about my wellbeing, but that's hard to believe when I recall her reporting my parents to the authorities and other hurtful things she's done and said to me throughout the years. But, no matter what, her commentary was more about her than me. I didn't take it personally then and I don't take it personally now. I've never claimed to be perfect and I know I'm not, but I'm striving to live my life to the fullest, aiming toward virtue and goodness, working toward the perfection of love—for my family, my friends, and my (future) husband. There is nothing to be ashamed of in living a life of chastity, which ultimately means that you are striving toward that perfection of love. And striving doesn't stop when you're being attacked for your beliefs, or when you go to Austria, or even when you get married. We should always aim to love others in the most perfect way.

In retrospect, even though I recognize that my aunt's attacks probably were more about her than me, I still felt embarrassed, confused, and shaken. To me, sex is personal and intimate. I've never been one to talk about it casually. However, like Aunt Alice, Patricia grew up during the sexual revolution. Like so many other young women during that time, they felt freed from the bonds that prior to that time had shackled women. They were taught to believe that sex was a way to freedom. Thinking about their personal history, maybe both Patricia and Alice perceived my convictions as the same outdated moralism that shackled previous generations. But to me, my convictions have always provided freedom, and in fact my decisions have protected me from a great deal of heartbreak and pain. My convictions have allowed me to live out the feminist dream, to live out all my dreams to the fullest.

For sure, my public exchange with Aunt Patricia stripped away my shyness or awkwardness when talking about sex and chastity. That conversation, that exchange, led me to see that living a life of chastity, although very personal, is a decision I could and should talk about openly, positively, and confidently. If people can talk flippantly and casually about hookups, one-night stands, and sexual escapades, why shouldn't we be able to talk honestly and directly about sexual integrity and chastity? My exchange with Patricia set the tone for many things I have said and written publicly throughout my life.

A year after that conversation, it came time to choose a thesis topic at Franciscan. I have always been interested in and intrigued by a variety of things: I'm a deep, pensive thinker with an interest in subjects that to some might seem trivial, like pop culture and celebrity gossip. So my first impulse was to write on how horror films are steeped in lessons on virtue. Deep down, they show that those who seek to live a virtuous life almost always survive. But the more I thought about it and discussed it with my thesis advisor (Fr. Dan Pattee, who is incredible! Shoutout to Fr.

Dan!), I decided to write on chastity. Conversations with peers growing up, conversations with concert goers during my summer with Stand True, my conversation with Aunt Patricia at the Christmas party, and many other exchanges with friends and family members throughout the years led me to explore the true and full understanding of virtue of chastity.

In "Chastity in the Modern World and the Fulfillment of Chastity within the Catholic Church," I examined views of sex and chastity in three contemporary contexts: Evangelical, secular, and Catholic. I sought to demonstrate that the fullest understanding of virtue, including the virtue of chastity, can be found within teachings of the Catholic Church. Chastity is often viewed as archaic, yet another prohibition on a long list of completely unattainable "don'ts" that are never practiced. But the more I researched and learned about chastity, the more I discovered that virtue embodies a beautiful list of "dos," not don'ts. Chastity, something stable and steadfast, has brought me freedom and allowed me to be my authentic self. Chastity is the perfection of love—not too much and not too little. Like all virtues, chastity is a process, a journey, something we should always be aiming toward. No one is perfect, but we should always be striving.

When I was fifteen my mom's dad, my grandfather Francis, passed away. I always felt a special connection to him, and to this day his life and words inspire me. The last time I saw him—a day or so before he died—he said something that has stuck with me about the beautiful journey of faith, virtue, and life. He said, "I'm just a work in progress." On his deathbed, hours before he passed away, my grandfather described himself as a work still in progress. I've sought to live by these words, to remember them as I pass through each chapter of my life. We should always be learning, growing, challenging ourselves, striving toward holiness and virtue, remaining open to learn from others.

As I look back on my teenage and college years, every conversation, every encounter, every experience has played a role in what has come about in my life, and what is still becoming. I'm still learning, still striving, and I hope—like my grandfather Francis—I will continue to do so until I leave this world. My past conversations with family and others have challenged me and inspired me and opened my eyes. And conversations that I have every day continue to do the same. Little did I know that the Christmas party exchange about chastity with Aunt Patricia or choosing to write my thesis on chastity were puzzle pieces that would fit together to create the picture of who I am meant to be and the things that I was born to do. Every experience, conversation, choice, encounter—positive or negative—every element in our lives is a part of our likeness, each piece fitting together with others to create a bigger, complete picture. Life has been a puzzle that I'm trying to assemble, but maybe I'm just supposed to collect the pieces, trust in the process, and let the picture puzzle of my life come together as I go. Now more than ever, I'm coming to believe that.

Chapter 4

Women Are Important—So Is This Journey Through Life

At the beginning of my senior year at Franciscan, my friend Amber told me about a recent "temper tantrum" with her boyfriend (soon after, her fiancé and now her husband). She reflected about how important it is for women to express themselves, even in frustration, because doing so makes it clear, especially to the men in their lives, that they have many layers, many dimensions, and how fascinating women are. As I recall, the tantrum—like most outbursts—was provoked by something insignificant, but Amber shared her story to encourage me and our friends to share our feelings, frustrations, joys, excitement. Women's intriguing complexity isn't always recognized or appreciated. Amber reflected on our many subtleties—in our person, our lives, and our hearts—and on our need to remind the world (including the men in our lives) of how captivating and important we are. She said, "Women are fascinating and it's important that our friends, boyfriends, husbands, and other men get to see all of our facets—to remind them of how fascinating and amazing we are." Women are fascinating, have many layers and facets, a beauty and uniqueness that should be celebrated. Amber laughed as she finished the story, saying how her boyfriend loved her even more every time she was authentically herself and expressed herself, even with a tantrum. As my life and career have unfolded, this simple exchange has stuck with me. I remind myself of what Amber shared, especially when I'm feeling salty or sassy.

I've always considered myself to be unique; another word that I might use to describe myself is "enigmatic." Honestly, we're all enigmas. We should recognize that and own it. What makes women fascinating is an enigmatic quality which reveals how we are beautiful, authentically human, the mystery each of us was created to be. Growing up we can strive not to draw attention to ourselves just to fit in, much like when I was a little kid and wanted to be invisible, just to get in line and not stand out. But everything that makes us unique—our appearance, our personality, our passions, our gifts and talents, our temper tantrums—all of it—make each of us fascinating, authentically us. Each of us is an enigma, and we should embrace it.

Life itself is enigmatic. Each life journey is one of a kind, a unique puzzle that's coming together day by day, one piece at a time. My mom always described people who embraced that journey as an adventure as "tasters of life." She was a "taster of life," as was my dad, and they encouraged my siblings and me to be tasters of life too. They urged us to chase our dreams, take chances, to seize every opportunity that crossed our path. I'm pretty sure I've accomplished that goal thus far, and I'm still tasting life every day.

I graduated college with a bachelor's degree in theology, never intending to teach theology or be a youth minister, nor did I feel called to religious life. Yet I always had a genuine interest in my faith and in scripture. After college, I moved back home and got a job working in AT&T's engineering department. I had no experience in engineering, but God is a God of miracles. My boss hired me because he said I had "people skills," apparently an unusual trait among engineers. I was grateful for the opportunity to have a good job that would allow me to pay off my mountain of student loans from Franciscan.

Like many chapters in my life, however, just as I started to hit my stride in this position, I came to another crossroads. I have always had a positive outlook. Perhaps because I suffered so much growing up, I've always been eager to embrace whatever opportunities, choices, or adventures life threw at me. Some people see life through a negative lens, but mine has always been positive. Some people see life as a series of unfortunate events that they hope will someday work out, but I've always seen it as a world of opportunity and an adventure. People sometimes seem to marvel at my life, how have I done so much in such a short time—traveling the world, working in numerous fields, experiencing so much. Honestly, though, all I've done is embrace the opportunities that came before me—no matter how edgy or crazy they may seem. Despite the edginess and craziness of my life, I have few regrets. At times I wish I had done things a little differently or that some things worked out differently, but I've learned to love and embrace every chance that's come my way. And at the end of the day, I have few regrets.

While I was at AT&T my life was about to take an unexpected turn toward politics and communications. I never had much of an interest in politics except as it touched on life and moral issues, but in 2008 everything changed. I was captivated by the presidential campaigns—Barack Obama and Joe Biden, John McCain and Sarah Palin—and by the all-consuming political conversation of the time. It was such an interesting election: so many firsts, so many questions, so many angles, and so many topics to discuss. I was enthralled. That election cycle I lived and breathed politics and put everything I was thinking and feeling into words. During those early years of social media, on Facebook people shared anything and everything and engaged in discussions and debates. Those were the days of social media "overshare," people sometimes posting too much, almost on the verge of silliness—like how they were feeling ("I'm sad"), or random actions ("I put too much paprika on my chicken"), or their faves ("I like donuts"). Sometimes I miss those days because now it seems as though you can't post anything, even a simple or funny thought, without someone taking offense or attacking you.

During those early days of social media, like millions of others, I turned my Facebook page into a personal blog. That's where my passion for political discourse and communications started percolating. Intrigued by political opinions and discussions, I wrote about whatever I was thinking and feeling. I wanted to learn the ins and outs of politics and political campaigns, as well as dialogue and discourse. Looking back, thinking about all the conversations and interactions I had with family members and others throughout the years, I see many influences that had led me to that moment. All those encounters and experiences paved the way toward the adventure I was about to embark on. Above all, I knew that whatever I decided to do with the rest of my life, I wanted to continue to grow and evolve—including in what I thought and what I believed. I wanted to learn from others, I wanted to be challenged, I wanted to be taught to think in new ways, I wanted to become a stronger communicator. Sitting at my desk in that windowless bomb shelter-looking AT&T building clicking away on my computer, my ache to be in the thick of political discourse grew stronger and stronger. Even after election day 2008 came and went, my interest in politics and communications kept intensifying. On Facebook I would post almost daily about what I was thinking and what I was seeing in the world, and people started to respond. In those early days, it was all close friends and family and people were respectful . . . more or less. Every so often someone would write a vitriolic response, but for the most part the commentary was interesting and fruitful. My posts and the conversations that those posts sparked reflected the way that things should be in our world—people had opinions, perspectives, and experiences, but were respectful and open, recognizing that others may have differing viewpoints. Every day I looked forward to these discussions. The more I thought about it and the more I engaged, the more I considered returning to school to study political communication.

I started looking at master's programs in the United States, but nothing resonated with what I was looking for. Most programs focused on reading and paper-writing, but I had always been more interested in applying my people skills to politics and communications. One night, while Skyping with a friend from Ireland (I visited Ireland a few times during my college semester abroad and kept in touch with friends there), he asked if I had considered going to a graduate school there. Before that moment I had never thought of it, but it made perfect sense to him. Graduate programs in Ireland were only one year long, cost a fraction of what I'd pay in America, and I would get international experience. It was perfect.

Having been raised in an Irish American family, I was well-versed in Irish culture, Irish people, Irish struggles throughout history, Irish politics and its political system. The more I balanced the pros and cons, the more sense it made. So I applied to a few colleges and universities in Dublin and when the Dublin Institute of Technology (the program I was hoping for) accepted me into its master's program in Public Affairs and Political Communication, I jumped at the opportunity. Within three weeks I quit my job, sold my car, and relocated 3,500 miles across the Atlantic.

This was another "suddenly" moment, when a door opened and I mustered the courage and gumption to walk boldly through. In some ways, the decision was easy. I moved to a country and city that I loved, I got to be around people that to this day I consider my second family, and I began working toward a career and life that I was excited about, one that I felt created for. But, as whimsical as a year (which ended up being over two) in Ireland sounds, it also had its challenges.

I had been straightforward in my interview with the chair of the program on what I thought and where I stood on life, faith, politics, and beliefs. In my conversations, I didn't shy away from divisive topics and stated clearly what I believed and why I believed it. As the first foreigner to go through the program I hoped that I would be welcomed, even if my beliefs didn't align with those of my peers and the professors. I don't think I was naive, but I did expect that my thoughts and perspectives would be encouraged and respected. Reflecting on my experiences at Ave Maria and Franciscan, I expected that bringing differing perspectives and opinions to classes would be encouraged. But quickly it became clear that I was an outsider, ostracized for my beliefs, my faith, even for my friends (I'm not kidding!). I was "encouraged" to get in line and regurgitate what was being taught.

At one point, very early on in the program, I was sitting in the office of the Life Institute, an Irish pro-life organization where many of my friends worked, when a protest erupted in the street outside. I ran to the window and saw a classmate, with a group of others, brandishing a placard attacking the organization for opposing the Lisbon Treaty, which would give Europe more power over Ireland. This is a topic that I would need another book to dissect, but I mention this story for a reason. I respected my classmate's freedom to stand up for what she believed. But the second she figured out that I was connected to the Life Institute in any way, she made it a regular point to challenge me in class and went out of her way to make sure I wasn't invited to class gatherings and events. When I was a little kid I was excluded from birthday parties because I had a rash. This was like that. Word began to spread through my program about my personal life and friendships, and I ended up getting a speaking-to by the program chair and a staff member from the Irish parliament (where I was interning that year). They ultimately told me to get in line. If I wanted to get through the program, I needed to stop affiliating with my friends at The Life Institute. These friends were good Catholics, standing up for their beliefs, yet they were disparaged by those in my program and I was ostracized, as if I were gallivanting around with criminals. I found it toxic and bizarre that my classmates could do whatever they wanted, yet I was spurned for grabbing a drink or dinner with my friends.

At some moments that year, I felt transported back to my seven-year-old self, when I had been ostracized for who I was (or who people thought I was), and isolated. And then of course those moments also brought me back to the experiences with my aunts or to instances when I was rejected or treated as if I were a disease. I realized that those life experiences had prepared me for something bigger, something like what I was experiencing in grad school. I realized, however, that I hadn't left everything behind back in Michigan, hadn't spent all this money and made so many other sacrifices to come to Ireland just to make new friends at the Dublin Institute of Technology. No, I took this step and made these sacrifices to learn, to grow, and to be challenged. Merely regurgitating what my professors said or what we were reading would go against everything that I am, everything I stand for, and everything I was hoping to become. I have never been a person who bows to someone or something that I know is wrong, and this program's specific aim was teaching us to become better communicators and leaders. While I have always tried to keep an open mind, I have also always been clear on what is true, what is right, and what is just. So, I decided to keep standing up.

Spoiler alert: I never stopped hanging out with my friends, never stopped speaking up for what I believed and standing up for those beliefs. I passed the program and have my master's degree in hand.

Taking a stand had its costs, but nowhere near what it would have been if I had muted myself to fit in with the status quo. Looking back, I think I would have lost myself, or at the very least pieces of myself. Had I bowed to the pressure I know that I would not be the empowered woman that I am today. I showed up to every class, to Irish Parliament every day when I was assigned there, always ready to participate, speak up, offer my perspective, and fight for what I knew was right and true. Some people may consider my time in Ireland merely whimsical, and in many ways it was. But overall it was hard work; each day felt like a battlefield. School and parliament seemed like a no-man's-land where I had very few allies and friends. But I did receive a great gift—the friends in Ireland that I had met during my previous college semester abroad became my second family. They were my reprieve, my resting place; during the craziest moments of my program they kept me sane. I always had someone to grab a beer with, a family where I could take refuge in a home-cooked meal, people that supported me and loved me throughout my time in Ireland. I learned some great lessons: never bow to the pressure of becoming someone that you're not; treasure true friends, love them, and hold them close. True friends are rare gems that you don't find often. So when you stumble upon one (or in my case, a whole Irish clan of them), hold them close.

During my time in Ireland I learned so much about myself and gained new perspectives on the world. One of those new perspectives has to do with the pro-life cause and the issue of abortion. And now, nearly a dozen years later, this still influences what I believe. As you know by now, I grew up in a family that had a deep reverence for all human life and I had my own experience of almost being snuffed out while still in the womb. During my two and a half years in Ireland, abortion was illegal. Ireland has since legalized it, but I will never forget the experience of living in a country that was abortion-free. Ireland's example during that time should be examined and regarded. While abortion was banned, Ireland had one of the lowest maternal mortality rates in the world and was one of the safest places for women to have a baby. Ireland was a center of excellence for women's healthcare and maternal healthcare. The pro-life movement was exemplary as well, their "activism" centered around mothers as well as their preborn babies in a way that the pro-life movement elsewhere should emulate. I was always struck by Ireland's slogan, "Love Them Both," and the equality in all that they did, promoting the best care and support both for pregnant women and for their babies. The pro-life cause in America and around the world can often be so focused on the baby that women get overlooked, ignored, and marginalized. I have always held a more wholistic view—wanting to protect all human life, including support and care for women— so Ireland's pro-life movement really resonated with me. There are many more aspects to this and much more I could say, but Ireland was a beacon, an example to the world of what women's healthcare and true pro-life endeavors should look like.

This chapter of my life shifted me toward politics and opened my world more than I expected, and until recently more than I realized. I did discover a love for politics and political discourse, but even more it opened my eyes to the corruption and brokenness of politics. I had placed great emphasis on the power of politics and politicians, but during my time in Ireland I came to realize the limitations of political power and of politicians themselves. And now more than ever I have come to realize that politics and politicians cannot save us. We should stop placing so much emphasis on politics, so much hope in politicians. It's up to us to be the change we want to see in the world. Through our lives we have the power to change the world. That's where the real power lies—with us.

I completed the master's program at DIT and stayed an additional year to work on my dissertation and spend more time in politics and advocacy. The one-year program itself was incredibly intense, and the adversity added another dimension of stress and difficulty. So I decided to stay longer, work on the projects that I wanted to, and enjoy my time in that country I so dearly love. That year I worked on numerous critical issues including suicide, assisted suicide, hospice care, poverty, homelessness, mental health, women's health, and more. But after two years away I started to feel a pull back to the States. I loved living in Ireland and had been building a life there, both personally and professionally, but I knew it was time to move back home. I had gone to Ireland to gain knowledge, experience, and perspective, but my focus never left America. I wanted to return, to fight for the American people and through the next chapters of my life and career to implement what I had learned. At the end of 2011 I left Dublin for Washington, DC to pursue a career in advocacy and communications.

I had always figured that at some point I would spend time in Washington and being in my late twenties, a master's degree in hand and still single, I decided to dive into this next chapter. I never fathomed that I would stay in the nation's capital for over six years. I still have some dear friends there, and my time and experiences in DC made me grow in ways I did not anticipate. I never worked in the White House or on the Hill, but instead focused on broader communications. I wanted to challenge myself by working for a variety of organizations and companies, and to continue evolving in my world-view and experience. At first I focused on life issues, but ended up getting experience on many, many topics and issues including education, monetary policy, immigration, health, and pizza (!!!). I worked in communications for nonprofits, as well for big corporations. Doing that elevated my knowledge and experience and has continued to help me to broaden and deepen my view of the world. I was challenged by the companies I worked with, my colleagues, and the many people from all over the world that I encountered. Interesting people are always passing through Washington—you never know who you might run into or who you might meet at a happy hour. Those years were really fun and formative.

Each year in DC continued to build on the foundation in education and experience that I had already established. But the longer I worked in communications and politics, the more my eyes were opened to the corruption and brokenness of political systems in America and around the world, and to the brokenness of humanity itself. I am grateful for the jobs I had and the colleagues I worked with, some great (you know who you are!) and some not-so-great (you also know who you are!). But the real value of my first-hand experience in DC was how it opened my eyes not just to the limitations of politics and politicians, but even more to my own purpose in life, my passion for people. At times what I saw and experienced disheartened me deeply, and even now when I hear about what's going on in DC, what some self-described "moral" people are doing, I cringe. Washington, DC is a bastion of the lost. So many have lost their way, have lost sight of what is right and true. That's not to say that there aren't good folks in DC; there are, and I know many of them. But there is such corruption even among Catholics and Christians, communities that have a responsibility to be better. Seeing the decay firsthand taught me that true power lies in the hands of the people. It's up to us to be the change we want to see in the world. I moved to DC to work in politics, but my time in the District expanded and changed my understanding of what the term "pro-life" actually means—or, rather, what it should mean. Even among advocates for "human dignity" and "life," I found individuals and organizations that did not promote the values and dignity they claimed to uphold. Some were actually repulsive. For some, "pro-life" meant advocating only for preborn children—not born children, not women, not fellow advocates, not their employees, not other human beings. My experiences made me lose respect for some who claimed to be "pro-life" and made me refocus on what matters to me and how I could act more wholistically to affirm and to respect every single human being. More than ever, I'm passionate about promoting *all* life. And about practicing what you preach. Talk is cheap.

Even though none of us is perfect, each of us has the responsibility to do everything we can to promote human dignity in all aspects, especially if we claim to promote it in our lives and through our work. Every aspect of our lives should reflect what we believe and stand for. We should be working constantly to improve how we live our lives and how we treat others. We're all imperfect, but we can strive to be better. We should constantly ask ourselves "check-in" questions about how our lives are reflecting our values. Am I honoring my friends and family? Are we paying workers a just wage? Do we create environments that support their health, wellness, and family life? Do we tip service workers well? Are we kind to those we encounter, even in the most stressful and difficult situations? Do we care equally about mothers and their children (unborn and born), the elderly, those with disabilities, immigrants, those who look different from us, those who think differently than us? If we believe that every life is precious and sacred, we should reflect that in every aspect of how we live our lives.

I often joke about "doing my time in DC" as if I had served a prison sentence, but I always intend that comment somewhat seriously. I met some of my dearest friends in there but also was burned by people who I thought were friends. On the whole, living and working there was a rocky experience, but it continues to shape me into the person that I'm still becoming. I have many fond memories of my time in DC and would certainly consider moving back temporarily, but I definitely saw far too much ugliness and corruption to make it my home. My time there opened my eyes to the hypocrisy of humanity, including my own. I recognize my own hypocrisy and every day I strive to be better, as each of us should be striving every single day to become better. I don't claim to be perfect. I know I have many flaws, as all of us do. We should recognize them, own them, and be better. One of my Irish friends used to say, "The worst thing in the world you can be is a liar." And lying means more than speaking what's not true; it also means living what's not true. My deep connection to faith compels me to seek the good and live a life of virtue. Christianity doesn't require people to be perfect. We never will be (except in heaven —holla!). But our faith compels us to be constant works in progress. To strive for something better. To live out the gospel more fully in our daily lives. All of us have sinned and we're constantly falling short of the glory that God created us for, but that shouldn't keep us from striving for that glory. Do I strive for that? Am I doing God's work? Do I invoke God's help and guidance as I seek to be the change I want to see in the world? These are questions we should consistently be asking ourselves.

A friend of mine was fond of saying, "What we do in the small things, we do in the big things," usually referring to me when I was late or forgot to do something I had committed to. I used to hate when he would say it, but it has become almost a daily mantra, a simple phrase I live by every day. I've used it in breakups (how someone treats you in small ways will play out in the big ways down the road), pay negotiations (you can talk about human dignity all day long, but if you're not paying your workers a just wage or encouraging them to have a good life-work balance, are you promoting human dignity?), and many other occasions. When I've used that phrase the person I'm talking to usually reacts like I did when I first heard it—they hate it. But I hope that they come to the same conclusion that I did—that it's true.

· When we were little my maternal grandfather, Francis, used to tell me and my siblings and cousins that in the house we could do anything we wanted to—fight, cause havoc, throw tantrums, anything—but the second we left the house we became a reflection of ourselves, our family, our faith, our beliefs, everything we stand for. So when we left the house we needed to remember what we were representing. And I too have come to believe that. My grandpa would say it with a wink, but we knew he was serious.

More than ever, we have the responsibility to set a good example in how we treat others, how we treat our family and friends, how we treat our spouses and kids, how we live our lives. We have the responsibility to be consistent in what we believe and what we stand for, how we live our lives, how we run our businesses, how we treat others. Indeed, no one is perfect, but every single day we should take this responsibility seriously and strive toward perfection. We all have flaws and we all struggle, but we should always keep striving. Day in and day out we should be consistent in what we're preaching, teaching, and representing. We are all important—and fascinating.

Chapter 5

"I'm a Thirty-two-year-old Virgin, Living the Feminist Dream"

As I said before, Washington, DC was an interesting chapter in my life. Bad things did happen to me—corruption, heartbreak, and disappointments—but we've all experienced those and will experience more such difficult things as we continue through life. But also, many good things did happen and that's what I wish to focus on now—the good over the bad. One of the best things that came out of my time there was the opportunity to grow my courage. Sometimes I had to stand up and speak out against injustice, to call out people doing inappropriate things, and sometimes I had to stand up even taller and speak louder than ever about the things that I cared about. I would joke that I always loved a good protest (I still do!). Whenever there was a demonstration about an issue that I cared about, I was there. And while Michigan offers many fewer opportunities than DC does, I still love a good protest—and I always want to be a person that stands up and speaks out against injustice. During my time in DC, I learned new ways of speaking up for myself and what I believe, particularly in writing. It has always provided an outlet for expressing ideas I am thinking about and topics I care about, usually pop culture and virtue in modern culture. Even though writing has never come easy for me (even though I'm sitting here writing this book! A big shoutout and thank you to the editors!), I've always had a lot to say. Although I did offer to write an article for the *Washington Post*, I never sought to be a spokesperson or poster child for chastity.

Now, before I get to the article itself, let me answer a question many have asked me. Do I still stand by what I wrote? Some people suppose I may have changed my mind about chastity or that my views have evolved, a supposition that I guess is possible, especially since my views on other issues have evolved over the years. But with the *Washington Post* piece, I still stand by every word. The only thing I might have changed is to clarify that I am not saving kissing for marriage, as some readers of the article understood—or *mis*understood, depending on how you look at it. I've never spoken or written flippantly just to gain notoriety. I have to be really passionate about something in order to write anything. Which is exactly what led me to write the *Washington Post* article, as well as this book. Some people thought that I wrote the *WaPo* chastity piece just to get attention, which I laugh about because OF ALL THINGS I might write to get attention or to get a byline in a major daily newspaper, the very last would be chastity. As I've said before, sex is deeply personal and intimate to me. To talk about sex and chastity in such a public way opened me up to criticism and even danger (some men responding to the article said that they hoped I got raped). If I wanted attention, I definitely would've chosen a topic that didn't expose me on such a personal level. As for changing my mind, I guess that's possible—but to me that doesn't really make sense. I have come to a deeper, fuller appreciation of chastity—saving sex for marriage and the perfection of love—and that's not going to change. I've lived this way for thirty-six years; why would I give up now? I've come too far and now I know too much. I have come to such a deep understanding of chastity as the perfection of love that I could never give myself fully and completely to someone outside of marriage. So to answer those with inquiring minds, I still stand by every word I wrote in the *Washington Post*.

I have read articles and books attacking "purity culture"—there are many of them—and I agree with many of the concerns they raise. Joshua Harris's book *I Kissed Dating Goodbye* and many other Evangelical authors (and, honestly, many Catholic and even secular authors) do not get this topic right. They do not fully connect sex and respect for our fellow humans, especially the ones we love. If we truly live out chastity, on the other hand, we promote authentic love and respect for every human we encounter, and demand from others the same respect for us. I don't claim to be an expert on authentic love and respect, but in recent years I haven't seen much that really captures what chastity is and what it's not.

I began my own experience with purity culture during my teenage years, jumping in completely with "The Chastinator" and my chastity ring, but I did not begin to understand the complete meaning of chastity until I was in college, and then even more so as an adult. In college, reading John Paul II's *Love and Responsibility* transformed my thinking on chastity, bringing me to begin comprehending the totality of the virtue. He writes that "a person must not be merely the means to an end for another person," something all of us unfortunately have felt and many still feel regularly. And maybe that's how we, ourselves, have often treated others. On social media we are a mere number; in politics we're a statistic; even in our daily life we're treated as a means to an end. And, unfortunately, we too contribute to the problem because we can treat those we encounter as a means to an end. Do we treat the person at the coffee counter or the person serving our food at a restaurant as a human being, or is that person just the means to get what we ordered? Do we walk through life alongside our friends and family or do we use them transactionally to fill a void in our lives? We've all felt used and abused, and in fact throughout our lives *we have been used and abused*—in romantic relationships, at times during sex, in hook-ups, in friendships, and in tragic encounters. Sometimes we are the culprit that inflicts abuse. Too often in the broader culture people are considered merely as instruments, after which they become "disposable." But we can change this. In our own world we can treat each person we encounter with the love and respect they deserve.

Throughout my life I've experienced this in many ways. In some instances, I thought someone was a friend, but found out that they were just using me to connect with someone else or for professional gain. Like everyone, I've also had "friends" who call or want to meet up only if they need something. Such "friends" will be there for us during the fun parts of our lives, but probably not when we're struggling. That's not friendship. Real friendships and relationships are intentional. Any small intentional action on our part contains the power to change the world. Throughout the day, in every little interaction, each of our fellow human beings deserves respect. So that means no road rage. LOL.

And this is where chastity comes in. If we focus on attempting to love others in the most perfect, honest, and authentic way, seeing each other as fellow human beings instead of as the means to an end, the world would look a lot different. This has always been the lens I've looked through with regards to chastity: "Am I loving the other person in the most perfect way?" "Is this the best expression of love?" This was also the lens through which I was reading the *Washington Post* articles that provoked my response. I understood some of the authors' critiques, especially that purity culture can sow fear and shame regarding sex, but I found myself thinking, "This isn't the full story." I would never denigrate others' experiences, but as I read those pieces, I found myself reflecting on my own life journey and finding it to be the opposite of theirs. Chastity offered me freedom. And I know many others who have felt that same freedom. Even those who had been sexually active, when they committed (or re-committed) to chastity, found a new freedom. As I read those two pieces in the *Washington Post*, I found myself thinking about all the people I know who have lived lives of chastity, who have committed or re-committed themselves to chastity. We've felt a great deal of freedom. We didn't experience the "shackles'" that these authors said they experienced, as it happens—according to them—to everyone who chooses chastity or abstinence. So, that sunny August morning I decided to sit down and write a response on my own behalf and on behalf of many others, never imagining that this piece would get published.

The moment I opened the email from the *Washington Post* is tattooed on my memory. The editor said that the *Post* planned to run my article and asked me to suggest a title and to send a picture of myself to be included with the piece. My roommate at the time (who remains one of my closest friends) and I laughed hysterically over what I should submit. A lot of people have preconceived notions about what someone who lives a life of chastity would look like and we laughed ourselves to tears considering photo options I could send. Our world is visual, and it's rare to see someone in her thirties who would say publicly that she's never had sex. It was one thing to be a sixteen-year-old with a bumper sticker on "The Chastinator" that said, "Chastity is for Lovers," but quite another to be proclaiming the same thing half my life later. We joked about Googling "cat lady" or "lady in plaid jumper who lives in her parents' basement" and choosing the most ridiculous image we could find. I ended up sending a couple of options, but both were me, looking like a normal, thirty-something professional living in Washington, DC. I left it up to the editor to choose, never imagining the power of a simple photo to shape people's perceptions, or what that photo would trigger. I'm not a unicorn. There are many others out there with beliefs and experiences like mine, but the day my picture and my piece ran in the *Washington Post* I definitely felt like a unicorn (or circus exhibit, LOL!).

As for the title, I considered various creative options, but finally concluded that I should be clear and direct. In communications sometimes it's best, even in conversations, to cut straight to the chase and say exactly what you mean. There are times to be clever and savvy, which is honestly one of my favorite strategies (especially working in public relations) but sometimes it's best to be straightforward and honest and throw a fastball right down the middle to see what the public will do with it. So I wrote "I'm a 32-year-old virgin, living the feminist dream," and clicked "send "on my email back to the editor.

Some found that title provocative, but I intended it to be simple and direct. I loved how "I'm a 32-year-old virgin, living the feminist dream" embodied the truth of what I described in the piece. I honestly believe that the way I've conducted my life has allowed me to live out the feminist dream. Actually, "believe" is too weak a word here. I *know* that the way that I've lived my life has allowed me to live out the feminist dream.

"Feminism" is often spoken about in the context of politics, abortion, and the sexual revolution, but in reality feminism is about advocating for women's full equality, rights, and freedom. And those three things include many facets of each woman's identity and what brings her true equality, true rights, and true freedom. Women are fascinating, complex beings, reflected in who we are and how we live our lives. But imagine the freedom of women who don't spend their days fretting about someone else's intentions, or where they stand, or stressed because they hooked up and could be pregnant or had sex with someone who never called them back. Women (and men!) experience such things every single day, and living out chastity can safeguard us from painful insecurity and uncertainty. I have always believed (and still do!) that women are at our best when we feel stable, safe, and secure— when there is no question about where we stand and what's going on in our lives. Throughout my life I've been empowered when I felt stable, safe and secure, and I know other women would agree. Abortion is often touted as a source of women's freedom, but it's always concerned me deeply that "feminism" would be connected with violence. Abortion is a violence against women and their children. Women deserve better. We should support women and their children, empower women, and end violence against women (for that matter, violence against anyone).

My *Washington Post* article explains how chastity allows women (and all people, truly) to gain true equality and freedom. I'm not saying that chastity is merely the absence of sex. Realistically, many people will not *not* have sex outside of marriage. And now, with dating apps, hookup apps, and all the blurred lines of how people interconnect, dating and relationships feel more complicated than ever. I won't venture to break down the entirety of what is going on with all those different dimensions of intimacy, but I will say that much of the confusion comes back to how we view sex. And, in reality, to how we view chastity. Free will allows humans to do whatever they choose, but that ability seems to have gone so far as to facilitate people hooking up, using each other, ghosting each other, and then realizing that they have to deal with the consequences. Relationships have many nuances and each one is unique, but if the virtue of chastity was understood and practiced I think the world of intimacy would look a lot different—and better. Hear me out. I recognize that not everyone will refrain from sex before marriage, but if every person—even those who are sexually active outside marriage—sought to practice the virtue of chastity, to strive to love others in the most perfect way, they might find themselves changing the way they approach sex and relationships, or even deciding to make a permanent commitment to their partner. At the very least, practicing the virtue of chastity would open them up to a new freedom.

In my own experience, my commitment to chastity—that is, striving to love others in the most perfect way—has sown the seeds of freedom and empowered me in numerous aspects of my life—not just in romantic relationships. Of course, there are social constructs that still constrain women's equality and we must continue to challenge and change those structures, but chastity addresses many of the forces that hold women back. A commitment to chastity challenges others—especially intimate partners—to treat you with respect, to love you authentically and deeply, and to focus on who you are as a person instead of what gratification they can get from your body. It also helps us as women to see others in the same light and love them in the most perfect way, focus on communication, build a strong foundation, and allow the time and space to determine whether this is the right person with whom to make a permanent commitment. Relationships are complex enough; taking sex out of the equation and focusing on establishing a strong foundation and on communication only strengthens the possibilities and simplifies the complexities. We could get into the divorce rates in our world (over 50%) and the broken relationships that seem to be caused by lack of communication. Even in marriage people haven't learned to converse. Practicing the virtue of chastity (striving to love the other in the most perfect way) opens up space for communication. The virtue of chastity in marriage doesn't necessarily mean not having sex; rather it's a broadening out of striving to love the other person in the most perfect way. Many marital problems stem from getting swept up at the beginning in romance and emotions, without focusing on how to build a long-lasting relationship and love connection. When the starry eyes disappear and life gets hard, the marriage falls apart. Whereas committing to chastity is a consistent invitation to both partners to love each other in the most perfect way and to keep striving to do so throughout their lives.

On September 8, 2016, the day that the *Washington Post* published my piece, I woke up to a flood of email messages, texts, and mentions on Twitter. Apart from the publication of the piece, this date (unbeknownst to my editor) has another special meaning for me. As I mentioned before, I've always looked to Mary, particularly Our Lady of Guadalupe, as an icon of resilience, peace, courage, and strength. September 8 is Mary's birthday, an important day for everyone—and not just Catholics—who honor her as the Mother of God. One of my sisters, a cousin, and one of my godsons were born on September 8, making the day even more meaningful for me. I knew that God might have something significant up His sleeve with this piece, but when I realized that it was going to run on September 8, I was like, "Buckle up because this ride is about to get crazy!" I knew that God had big things planned.

When the article came out, I wasn't sure what response I would get. I thought friends and family would probably support me. I'd probably get some haters, but some people would connect with it and stand with me. Again, I didn't really know what response to expect, but it ended up being very different from anything that I ever could've imagined.

At first, I felt like I was standing alone, but I remained steadfast and tried not to pay attention to the haters. If you're convicted and feel confident that you're doing the right thing, sometimes you have to stand alone, and that's OK. Standing alone definitely is not easy, but at those moments I believe we become even more authentically ourselves. We don't focus on what others think about us or trying to please others. We have no choice but to be confident in our own skin, stand alone in our convictions, and embrace our enigmatic selves. There's something beautiful and powerful about these moments. They definitely won't be easy, but if you embrace such moments I promise that your life will be more authentic, more meaningful, and often full of unexpected blessings.

The first comments I received came from friends and others around the country (and around the world!) who I knew or had worked with over the years. Right off the bat, I received some really beautiful notes of support from people who said that they agreed with what I wrote and were happy that the *Washington Post* ran it. But very quickly the piece went viral. And the farther it went, the more comments came in, and the more diverse the responses became. The headline was definitely intriguing, and because papers around the world ran the piece with the photo of a normal looking girl (not a cat lady— ha ha!), the article continued to gain steam. The piece ended up going so viral and provoked so many strong reactions and the responses flooded in so quickly that the *WaPo* website had to turn off comments.

After such initial massive support and interest, like so many things in life there was a flip side. If you're a person of faith with a biblical perspective you may believe that Satan attacks things that are good and even targets your friends, family, career, your whole life. Others may believe that there is evil in the world and whenever you're doing something good you must be prepared to be a target of the darkness. I've experienced such moments throughout my life but reading the negative feedback to this article was one of the most painful experiences I've ever endured. I was used to family and friends disagreeing with me, but the backlash to this piece took disagreement to a deeper, darker place.

There were Christians who said it wasn't Christian enough, Catholics who said it wasn't Catholic enough, and some who said it was too Catholic or too Christian. Some aggressive self-proclaimed feminist writers and commentators said that I couldn't possibly be a feminist, that I must be one of those women from A *Handmaid's Tale*. Honestly, I got the most bizarre commentary from all angles, all shades of the spectrum.

Not surprisingly, many vitriolic responses came from strangers—and most were from men. Unfortunately, this is the reality of today's online experience. I had published articles in the past and had learned not to take online commentary too personally or too seriously. I learned to let harsh comments roll off my back because I recognized that these people didn't actually know me and that their "arguments" usually didn't have much substance. It was often name-calling or mocking my life, beliefs, or appearance. The response to my *WaPo* piece wasn't much different. Most of the worst messages came from men. Some seemed to feel I had attacked them personally and sent violent threats, attacking me and my looks, or hoping someone would rape me so I would "know what I was missing." Disturbing. Other guys called me "gross" or "lame" or made nasty comments about how I looked. One wrote that my eyes looked "crazy," and another said I was "fat" and "no one would ever f**k her." Throughout my life I had dealt with commentary about my appearance, especially because of my eczema, but to receive judgments about my body from men around the world was really unnerving. I've always found comments about another person's body to be repulsive, particularly when men say things about women's bodies. To me, that is one of the ultimate and most profound disrespects against women.

Why did some men take it personally and feel compelled to attack? Perhaps because my message was one of empowering women who could challenge their access to casual hookups. My article empowered women to say "no" and stand up for themselves and take a stand for sexual integrity. Umm, hello #metoo! It's interesting to consider that a year after my article ran in 2016, the MeToo movement (which was founded ten years earlier, in 2006) gained momentum, exposing the horrifying sexual assaults by Hollywood icons like Harvey Weinstein and Bill Cosby, and opening the doors for women to step forward and speak up about sexual abuse and assault. While that was not the topic of my article, my story is the flipside of the same coin. My voice and my story were met with the same harassment directed to all the courageous women who came forward and spoke up about sexual abuse. Men wanted to stifle my voice and my experience(s) too. MeToo. Perhaps my challenge to the way they looked at the world intimidated these men; most definitely I challenged the way they looked at women. Whatever it was, especially in the context of writing a book on "the Feminist Dream," it's important to note that the most vile, inappropriate, degrading comments I received came from men.

It is also worth noting that I also received messages from guys who expressed genuine respect for my choice of chastity. I even got some invitations to go out on dates. I'm sure that some of those guys saw my commitment to chastity as a challenge, like in the movie *Cruel Intentions*, but overall, I encountered some men who seemed really genuine good guys who were encouraged by the vision I put out there.

(Note to all the women reading this: Hey girls, I just wanted to take a moment to encourage you to be exactly who you are, know what you stand for, and don't ever be afraid to speak up and stand up. As I write this book I'm still not married, but I believe that when the time is right the best man for me and I will find each other. And I believe the same for you. When we become most authentically ourselves we are the happiest and most fulfilled, and that's when the best relationships

come to fruition. So don't give up hope and know that there is someone out there who is going to believe in you, support you, and love you for exactly who you are!)

I also received amazing support from all over the world, people I had never met but who agreed with me or at the very least respected my choices. Many women and girls reached out to say that they were striving to live like I did or had re-committed themselves to chastity and were striving to live that way now. Some simply wanted to say thank you, others who had made a similar decision wanted to express their solidarity. Others said that they finally felt "heard," that they weren't alone, that they felt empowered to remain strong and speak up. Some women said that they didn't agree with me about chastity, but that they respected me and my decision. Those were actually some of my favorite comments—a reminder that we don't have to agree with someone but can still respect them and their decision. The message I was offering elevated the voices of previously silent women and empowered them to speak up and to stand up. In turn the positive response was an energizing gift—a gift that to this day is still giving. Even now, years later, from time to time I still receive encouraging notes and comments related to this piece.

But as I said, there was a lot of negative backlash as well. The piece was all over Twitter, other social media, and it got picked up in publications around the world—with my picture and the tagline: "I'm a 32-year-old Virgin Living the Feminist Dream." I learned not to look at social media at night when I was by myself because the predictable yet still hurtful comments seemed to cut deeper. (And I've continued that rule of thumb with regards to social media. Looking at a comment or a tweet during the day, when I'm with other people and in the midst of life and have other things going on , doesn't bother me as much.) But, overall, I let such negativity roll off my back. I was able to keep my head on straight and remain firm in my conviction that I was living the feminist dream.

Easily the most difficult moments, however, came from those closest to me. It's easier to deal with strangers because you can ignore them, but when those you hold dear question you or attack your beliefs or something you wrote—that can cut the deepest. A few weeks after the piece ran a dear friend of mine met me for dinner at drinks at a beautiful outdoor cafe. Like me, Gabby and her husband are practicing Catholics and had faced their own public attacks because they were involved in politics and were vocal advocates for the teachings of the Church. We had walked through many difficult chapters of life together and I always tried to support them in all things. I hadn't heard anything from them since my piece ran but assumed they had been busy or agreed with the piece and didn't feel the need to respond. So at the very least, because of their own experience and because we had been friends for years, I thought they would at least support me in this moment.

The first part of our dinner was really nice, just catching up and chatting, but without warning the hammer came down. Gabby announced, "We read your piece . . . And we hated it." Sitting there, stunned . . . never in a million years thinking that someone so close to me would read my piece and say such a thing, or say it like *that*. She went on to tell me that I had "changed" and that a piece like this one was an example of how "surface level" I had become. She implied that I had written it to get likes or attention, perhaps as a publicity stunt. As I said before, if I wanted to write to get attention, I would've written a different piece and most definitely wouldn't have shared with the whole world something so personal and intimate. I've never been one to say or write anything because it might get people to like me more. I've always had a deep sense of discernment and conviction and that's where this piece sparked from: I thought about it, prayed about it, talked about it, and when I felt convicted to write it, well . . . I did.

At that cafe table with Gabby, I sat in shock as she continued to bash my piece and go on about how much I'd changed. Tears began welling up (I absolutely hate crying in public because when I cry, my face turns red and I can't talk) so I sat there and took it and I cried. I cried hard. While I thought she was wrong, what she said made me take a good, long, hard look at myself. I always want to become better; I'm always striving toward becoming a better version of myself. And more than anything, I didn't want to be one of the people who comes to DC and turns into the worst version of themselves. I'd seen it and experienced it with others and that was the last thing in the world I wanted to become. I took what she said to heart and began asking myself critical questions--even while sitting at dinner. Had I changed? What was my purpose in writing this piece? And why me? Why did I have to be the person to write this piece? Was I really supposed to write this piece? Should I not have written the piece?

Over the years I've written many articles, given many speeches, and said many things publicly. Friends and family have often disagreed with me, something I love and respect about them. But to have written something so intimate and to have one of my close friends make me feel embarrassed and ashamed—like I had done something wrong—and to be attacked personally was one of the most difficult things I've ever experienced. It's also worth noting here that as fulfilling and freeing as chastity can be, I have felt the ache of singlehood. It can be lonely. So to already be experiencing loneliness and wanting so desperately at times to find the person for me and then to share about my decision so publicly—and then to get attacked first by strangers and then by a friend—it was one of the most painful experiences of my life. Gabby could've brushed over my piece and said something like "It wasn't my favorite piece you've written" or "I didn't like it" or "It didn't really speak to me"—any of those would have been understandable, but to take it upon herself to be critical not just of my piece but also of me personally . . . that pierced me to the core. I cried a lot during that dinner and then cried the whole drive home. After that night, I spent the next few months soul-searching, really taking to heart what Gabby said and discerning if she was in fact right: had I changed? I talked with family and other friends to ask their honest opinion about what she told me.

My conclusion—and it's important that I share it with you—is that yes, I had changed . . . but not in the ways that Gabby described. I've changed a great deal since the *Washington Post* article came out, and since that night. We should always be growing and evolving, and that's a good thing. I talked to many close family and friends about Gabby's impressions because what she said really hit me hard. Especially those of us who come from the Midwest place an emphasis on staying authentic, even though that's often mistaken for resistance to changing from who you were growing up. The friends with whom I inquired said yes, that I had changed, but in good ways, in directions in which they hoped I would continue to grow and evolve. We should always be growing, evolving, changing—we should always be *becoming* who we were created to be. Just as my understanding of chastity had evolved since I was a teenager and I'm sure will continue to evolve when I get married and have a family. We should always be growing and evolving.

Thankfully, throughout the years everything I have experienced, conversations I have had, people I have met, have made me grow and evolve. That's what made me strong enough, bold enough, and courageous enough to write that *Washington Post* piece. Maybe my friend hadn't changed or evolved and felt "left behind," or maybe she was struggling with something else and it was easy to unload on me. But this instance challenged me and, as with so many other moments of adversity in my life, made me discover deeper compassion and love. We don't know what other people are going through or why they may attack us, but above all we have can choose to meet every person with compassion and love.

I share this story because there will be moments when you need validation and support, especially from your friends and those close to you, but sometimes you have to show up for yourself. And if you need someone else, look to a family member or friend—or to God— to hold you up when you're not strong enough to support yourself, or to stand with you when you're standing alone. Remain steadfast in who you are and what you stand for. Surround yourself with a tribe that has your back, people who love you no matter what. Remain true to who you know you are, who you were created to be, and who you are becoming. God created each and every one of us for a purpose; it's our responsibility to find out what that is and to chase that vision. There will always be people who won't understand, who won't "get it," even those who try to tear you down and distract you from your path.

But stand strong. And to me, above all, that's what living the feminist dream is all about. Listen to Catherine of Siena's idea: "If you are what you should be, you'll set the world ablaze." That's it. Chastity has given me the ability to be more authentically myself and to understand my mission and purpose in this world without the pressures that sex and other dimensions of intimate relationships can stoke. You were created for an incredible purpose, so no matter how you go about finding out what that is—whether you follow what I've shared or blaze your own path— realize who you were created to be. Don't be afraid to change or challenge the status quo. Your life will set the world ablaze.

Chapter 6

Women's March

Of all my years in the District the last couple were the most formative. During that time, running PR for some very prominent organizations opened my eyes to issues like immigration, economics, education, persecution worldwide, and many others. Those experiences made my vision evolve, just as, I honestly believe, our own lives should always be evolving. Indeed, I had strongly held beliefs but I wanted to continue to learn and grow and understand other perspectives. Working deep inside PR and media, I gained new understanding and perspective. I got to see firsthand, for example, that media blackouts do happen—when a blind eye is turned to stories that should be covered—and those blackouts reveal a lack of media integrity. I also learned that most reporters, producers, and media personalities try to cover the news with integrity, but often don't have all the facts or weren't given all the details. Recognizing those realities, I made it my personal mission to take every opportunity to meet with reporters, even if I thought their agenda might differ from mine, give them the benefit of the doubt, and become a resource and connector for them. One of my favorite things in life is making connections, so I loved directing reporters and producers to people who I knew or who might give them a new perspective or important facts. This is truly the job of PR professionals, to link people with those who can help tell the story in an authentic way, even though PR professionals—like reporters and the media—do have their own agendas and want to promote their own clients. Although I was promoting certain clients, I always maintained integrity in my work and above all sought to be a resource for reporters. If reporters messed up a story, or if it became clear that they had an agenda, I would call for a correction and address the issue with them. But overall, giving reporters the benefit of the doubt meant that some really amazing stories came out of our relationships. (Shoutout to my former boss who taught me about professional compassion and media integrity!)

One such story centers on the first Women's March, back in January 2017. This was around the time I began noticing that sometimes reporters weren't told the whole story or weren't given all the facts, so I started keeping my eyes open for stories and information that might interest reporters I knew, building relationships with them and working to promote integrity between PR and media by sharing relevant information that I knew or had come across, even if it wasn't connected with my own clients or projects. That's where my interest in the Women's March began.

In November 2016, right after Trump won the presidential election, I began seeing glimmers of a women's march popping up on social media. There wasn't even a website yet, just little murmurings about a women's protest/gathering in Washington, DC. Every mention I came across contained some semblance of "Come one, come all!" I was fascinated and found myself following everything that was going on, keeping my eyes out for more. And then, all of a sudden, at the end of December or very early January, "BAM!": a public page for "The Women's March" posted saying the event was taking place in Washington, DC on January 21, 2017.

Everything on the website suggested inclusivity—it seemed everyone was welcome, and this would be a moment for women's stories and their voices to be heard. I loved it! This was exactly what I felt that the world needed then and had needed for a long time. It was shocking that something like this had never been done before. Women's marches had taken place, definitely in DC, but they were always hyper-politicized and divisive; I thought for a moment that this could be *the march* to change all that. What the world needed then, and what it unfortunately still needs, is a place where people can come together. In the face of so much division, it was hopeful and energizing to imagine our power if all women could all stand together, even if we were focused on differing issues. I thought it was awesome that the organizers of the March seemed to be committed to our commonality and were creating an opportunity for women of all ages, backgrounds, creeds, issues, interests, and more to come together. To stand together. To march together.

I had been working on many different issues through the years, many of which had differing sides and viewpoints, so I remember thinking distinctly, "Wow! Imagine if we would bring women together—no matter what they stand for, what their issue of interest is, or where they came from—to stand together and raise up their sisters, raise up all voices, all issues, and all perspectives." POWERFUL! I haven't always agreed with the people and organizations I have worked with over the years, but I always loved it when we could come together, at times from differing viewpoints, to support one another and dialogue with one another. And that's what I had hoped for with the Women's March. At that point I had worked on so many different issues, many marked by discord and disunity, that it was almost intoxicating to imagine the power of women, even amid our disagreements, coming together as one. What if the March brought together the pro-common core mamas and the anti-common core mamas, those who were pro-immigration and those more focused on immigration reform, those fighting for criminal justice reform and others passionate about economic issues or climate change—or whatever issue they cared about most. What if the March brought together those who thought differently about abortion, economic issues, education, anything else you can think of! Imagine the power if women from across the nation came together, to stand together, and no matter what their issue joined arms! When women come together, even if they have differing views, incredible things happen. Imagine the power and the impact of coming together. That event and gesture could begin transforming the world. I was captivated by the possibility.

But the Women's March would play out in a very, *very* different way.

Around that time, I went for coffee with a renowned religion reporter—we'll call her Emma—who I have always admired and with whom I had worked on numerous stories. It was a blistering cold day in DC, and we met at Whole Foods. While we sat there in our coats, shivering the entire time and sipping our coffee, Emma shared stories she was working on or thinking about. In turn I shared my client list, story ideas, and my recent travels for a piece I was working on about teachers' unions. Maybe because I'm Irish and we all love to tell stories, I'm almost always thinking of stories to tell, stories that should be told, or stories that I wish someone would tell. There is no lack of stories, but there are definitely not enough hours in the day for reporters to tell all of them, so there often is a lack of opportunity for them to be told. So, I always kept a whole list of ideas in my head and was always looking for people, even outside of my client purview, who I could pitch them to. As we got to the end of our meeting Emma asked, "What's a story that no one is covering that I should be?"

I've lived through more than a few "suddenly moments," and this was certainly one of them. The first thing I thought of was the Women's March. I had heard from numerous friends from the pro-life community who were planning on participating. They wanted to be a voice for women and their unborn children, had seen what the Women's March organizers had posted —that everyone was welcome—and, like me, seemed to believe it. The March announcement said, over and over, loud and clear, that the March was open to everyone. Anyone who wanted to attend was welcome to bring a sign with their issue.

When Emma asked me what story she should be covering, I blurted out: "You should write about pro-life women joining the Women's March." For a second she stared at me blankly. And then, with a puzzled look on her face, she said, "Ummm, yeah, that's not a story. The Women's March has made it very clear where they stand on abortion." I responded, "There is not a single mention of the word abortion on their website or any of their promotions or anything else that they have out there." As I made my case she listened and then as we left the coffee shop, with skepticism in her voice, she said she would look at the website and circle back with me if she thought it was a story.

Less than twenty-four hours later, Emma called. She said, "I'm going to write the story." She asked who I recommended she speak to, and I immediately started connecting her with people. This is exactly how PR and media should work. I saw a story that wasn't being told, one that I felt deserved to be told, pitched the story, and although the reporter was skeptical, she did her due diligence and when she recognized that it really was a story, she chased it with an open mind and wrote a straight account that simply covered what was unfolding before our eyes.

Emma wrote about pro-life women joining the Women's March—some had already been accepted as official sponsors—and the second it ran a firestorm broke out. The pro-life women and organizations that had previously been accepted as sponsors were immediately disinvited and removed from the website, and the Women's March released an official statement of principles that now included a push for "reproductive rights" and abortion. And in case there was any doubt, they said directly that if you didn't follow their principles and get in line, you were uninvited and unwelcome.

Given that I have experienced such rejection my entire life, this was not surprising. If you're not cool enough or you don't fit in with the crowd, you're not invited. Typical herd mentality—get in line or get out. Have a skin condition or look different—uninvited. If you speak up for something that doesn't fit into the status quo or blaze your own path—uninvited. So, while not surprising, it was still deeply disappointing. The platform I had hoped for, one where all women (whatever their age, issue, creed, zip code, or cause) could stand and march together, where every person's voice and perspective would be heard, would clearly not be the Women's March. That kind of sisterhood, it seems, would take a real revolution.

The first Women's March drew approximately 600,000 people. I was one of them, but throughout the entire march all I thought about was, "Imagine the power if women actually stood together, stood together amid their differences of opinions and beliefs." I marched that day for all women and my priority wasn't political, even though the Women's March became incredibly politically charged. I think often about my experience with the March—noticing the story, interacting with the reporter, pitching the story, the story igniting the Women's March, specific women and groups being kicked out, and the March itself. My experience exemplifies what happens in our world every single day. It should challenge us to work toward a better future where women won't be separated, ousted, marginalized, silenced, or ignored. Every woman has a voice, has a story, and deserves to be seen and heard.

Women now are consistently divided, segregated, and politicized. I don't know about you, but I recognize this and I'm just so over it. I know that we are better than this, that we deserve better than this, and I'm holding out hope for a future where, as sisters, women can stand together and together be the change that we want to see in the world.

Chapter 7

Feminism

In my family feminism was second nature. My sisters, Delia and Moira, and I have lived our lives to the fullest. Our lives exemplify the "feminist dream," and how could they not with the example of our mother? I'll use this opportunity to say how inspiring my sisters and their lives are—Delia chased her dreams to live in Japan for a time, while Moira lived in Hawaii and went to art school. My sisters, just like my brother and my parents, inspire me daily.

My mom, in our eyes the original feminist, embodies everything that we wanted to be. As I mentioned earlier, throughout her life she had overcome a great deal of abuse and adversity and (against all odds) had become one of the first female telephone installers in the US. She travelled the world, lived a life that she chose, and then at thirty-four became an incredible wife and mother. In the early '80s most women got married young; my mom was an exception. She believed that she was a better wife and mother because she had lived a full life before choosing a spouse and having a family. Of course, not every woman waits until her thirties to get married and getting married young doesn't make you a better or worse spouse, but my mom's experiences led her to be the best mother and wife she could be. Many of my friends met the right person when they were in high school or college and felt ready to get married and have kids—and they're just as happy as my mom is. Everyone's journey is different, but my mom's is an authentic feminism story that I want to share with you.

Mary Agnes Cullen, born in 1948, lived through numerous life-changing chapters for women . . .and for the world. She and her seven brothers and sisters grew up in Detroit during the '50s and '60s. She tells stories about what she saw during that time through her family's windows. She and her siblings often joke (now) how every night they got to choose their entertainment—listening to the radio or watching the riots unfold in front of their house. According to her, they almost always watched the riots.

She went to Catholic school and tells the familiar stories of harsh treatment by nuns, which at that time sadly seemed to be the norm. Her family faced multiple financial crises. She also lived through a time when everything about rights—women's rights as well as civil rights—started to percolate. Growing up in a predominantly black neighborhood—she was the only white girl on her basketball team—gave her a unique perspective. She also grew up in a family that regularly welcomed neighbors, exchange students, anyone by themselves, to share a meal or spend the holidays with them. My grandparents raised their children to love everyone and to welcome all people. My parents raised us the same way.

My mom and dad also raised all of us to believe that we could accomplish anything and that every person—regardless of skin color, gender, faith, (or absence of it) or where they came from—had value and deserved upmost respect. Although it might sound like a cliché, or be dismissed as silly or naive, being raised this way had a powerful effect on our lives. Despite our often-humble circumstances, we were raised to believe that we could make a difference. Everything we did, even our small gestures, how we treated those around us, was important. We were taught to respect ourselves and others and to dream—to dream big. Yes, we would face adversity (my immune deficiency and other things in my early life certainly taught me that), but I was raised to believe I could achieve anything I put my mind to, to dream big, and that if I worked hard enough I could achieve those dreams. And I believed it. I still do.

In the 1960s the word "feminism" was catapulted to the forefront of public discourse. Betty Friedan's *The Feminine Mystique*, hailed as one of the most influential books of the twentieth century, is considered one of modern feminism's founding texts, but to me it has always had serious problems. Friedan promoted women finding personal fulfillment outside their traditional domestic roles, something I support and have personally lived out. But without nuance and openness to women choosing how they want to live their lives—including choosing to have both a family and a career—I worry that this conveys a limited, skewed version of feminism, one that unfortunately remains prominent.

Women today are often convinced to disparage the typical experience of their sisters from the 1950's—once you get married and begin having children your life and career as you knew it is over. This idea is incredibly judgmental but has become woven so deeply into the fabric of society that it's difficult for women to set their sights beyond having only one thing. As I've mentioned before, I grew up in a family that ingrained within me and my siblings that we can accomplish anything we put our mind to and that we truly can have it all—my mom is a perfect example. It's also worth noting that women shouldn't have to do it all. As a society we should do a better job supporting women in all of their choices—including choosing to continue a career path while having children.

It's no secret that, as women, our lives and stories are constantly politicized and wedges are driven to divide us. This is why I shared my story about the 2017 Women's March; it offered women the opportunity to draw together and promised equality, but instead politicized us and divided us according to the issues we care about, and by who we were perceived to be. This is hardly news to those who pay attention. Numerous factors have contributed to the politicization and polarization of women, but the leading causes include Friedan, the 1960s and 1970s feminist movement more broadly, and the sexual revolution. After the success of *The Feminine Mystique*, Friedan co-founded the National Organization for Women (NOW), which claims to promote women's rights but instead has maintained an agenda that politicizes and polarizes women. NOW's approach doesn't empower women; it separates us and holds us back. We are stronger together, but this organization, like many others, drives us apart.

In the 1970s, women like Jane Fonda and Gloria Steinem led the charge for so-called "women's rights." There were protests, marches, well-funded and coordinated media appearances, and political campaigns. They touted "women's liberation," but—then as now—did not ask critically and specifically about *what exactly they were liberating themselves—or us—from.* I agree that throughout human history women have been held back in many ways and often were treated as second-class citizens. Indeed, some of what Fonda, Steinem, and others claimed to be fighting against is still evident and prominent in the world today.

I celebrate the progress we've made and feel empowered and weep for joy when empowered women break through yet another glass ceiling. Empowered women truly empower other women. There are many who have inspired me, women like Oprah, Shania Twain, and Joan of Arc. I love stories of women who have used their platform to help other women realize their power and make a difference in the world. But while I celebrate empowered women and how far we women have come, I also recognize that we have much further to go and, in some critical ways, we actually have gone backwards.

Friedan and the feminists of the '60's and '70s fought hard against traditional "feminine" roles in the home. They blazed a path for women to have careers and lives beyond "barefoot and pregnant in the kitchen," but we are now realizing the cost of that transformation. Women now are encouraged to postpone marriage and are convinced that they must choose between career or family life, not have both. And society, our jobs, and the workforce as a whole are suffocating us with constant reminders of that. If a woman has a career, she is expected to invest herself in it completely and fully, with little to no space for a personal life. If and when she does marry, a woman is encouraged to focus on family life and often is coerced to believe that she can't have it all. And there is a double standard; men are expected to be fully invested in their careers and people swoon when a dad has to leave work early to get to a little league game. Women, on the other hand, are made to feel guilty (some of it is self-induced I'm sure) if they have to leave work early, and I've heard numerous women be questioned about whether or not they should continue working once they get pregnant. I have never heard stories like that about men.

Some of the onus falls on men. We need men to stand up and be better partners, husbands, and fathers by helping care for the house and the kids. Male bosses should encourage and empower women to recognize that they are capable of maintaining a career and a family and should support them in that journey. The world still acts as though women can't have it all, which on one level I understand. The reality is, we all have priorities that change throughout our lives, especially with marriage and children, but that doesn't mean we can't succeed in the world of work and succeed as wives and mothers.

After winning an award at the 2020 Golden Globes for her performance in *Fosse*, in her acceptance speech Michelle Williams famously advocated for abortion. She said, "I wouldn't have been able to do this without employing a woman's right to choose. To choose when to have my children, and with whom." Many in the pro-life movement were up in arms about her comments. Catholic speaker and former constant on *America's Next Top Model* Leah Darrow, responded to Williams' speech from a hospital bed while in labor to deliver her fifth child: "Babies don't kill our dreams; only abortion does." Pro-life activist and speaker Lila Rose tweeted, "Michelle Williams, while visibly pregnant, claims she wouldn't have won her #GoldenGlobes Award if she didn't kill her previous child. No trophy is worth more than a child's life." I understand their responses and I agree that the worth of human life cannot be compared to any honor or material award. Yet the nuances of Williams's comments made me reflect on what they actually convey about women in society today.

My conclusion goes beyond instant, Tweetable responses to her statement, whether from pro-choice or pro-life advocates. The reality is— in many ways Michelle Williams is right. Of course Williams has money to hire nannies and any other support that she might need, but as a mother she does have responsibilities that could have hindered her from winning the award and having the career that she's led. We could play the blame game or dissect and discuss her life choices and what led her to where she is, but at the end of the day, for me the bigger issue here is that Williams's story is the story of so many women. And as a society we have not done enough— at times it feels like little or nothing is being done—to provide a path for women to be truly supported, in all areas and aspects of their lives, so they truly can do it all.

Keira Knightley also received attention for something she said shortly after becoming a mother, upon winning a Hollywood Film Award for her appearance in *The Imitation Game*. A reporter asked how she balances it all and Knightley simply replied, "Are you going to ask all the men that tonight?" It was a simple clapback, but this interaction reflects how many individuals and society as a whole often view women. Even the "enlightened" entertainment industry doesn't believe in the power of women to have and do it all. And there isn't a single formula that fits each situation. We need to do better to support women throughout the various stages of their lives, we need to change the usual way of thinking that leads women to doubt that they can manage a career and a family, and we—especially as women—need to take a deeper look at comments made by women like Williams and ask ourselves what we're doing to support and encourage our sisters.

Everyone can take part in encouraging women at every stage and chapter of their lives to pursue their dreams and to believe that they can have it all. Instead of vague notions of empowerment and liberation, it is important to focus on what truly matters, on the goals we're actually fighting for, and not get tied up in the politics and division that make us deviate from that vision. Empowered women can live full authentic lives, chase their dreams, and achieve everything they want in life, be it a family or a career or all the above. Many women who are engaged mothers and wives have fought hard to build great careers, to have equal opportunities, and to be paid the same as their male counterparts. Women are fascinating. We have been created in such a way that we can balance whatever we can hope for and dream of. I wish the world would recognize this, but even more I wish that we ourselves would recognize this, embrace it, and live it out in how we, as women, treat ourselves.

I find the absolute best example of an empowered woman in Mary, the Mother of Jesus. Yes, she was a mother and a wife, but she was also a leading member of the community, engaged with her family and friends. She surely had to set her priorities and learn how to navigate all the aspects of her life, throughout her entire life. I envision her as a loving mother figure to everyone she encountered, a full and complete woman who radiated love and light. And at the root, at the very heart of feminism, that's what every woman is called to be. That's what resonates with others. If we are the women we were created to be, be it as a mother, wife, friend, sister, entrepreneur, career woman, or whatever we feel called to do, we will radiate love and light to others and empower other women (and men!) to be the person they were created to be. As their circumstances change, of course, women have to learn to prioritize, but it can be done. The world needs women to be wholly who they are created to be.

Some success stories also show how far we've come. In recent years one phenomenon brings to light the power women have when they stand together: the culture-shifting awareness of, discussions about, and policy shifts concerning sexual assault. Sparked by the #MeToo movement, an army has been raised up. Long before such violence was widely documented, countless women (and men too!) suffered in silence and buried their trauma and grief after lifetimes of abuse and assault. But since 2017, when the accusations against Harvey Weinstein and others became public, many—including a veritable army of women—have found their voices and the courage to stand up and to speak up. This is what true feminism looks like—the social force of women standing together and empowering one another. As the saying goes, "Empowered women, empower women."

Even though some argue that the #MeToo movement has been politicized, this movement is worth honoring because it creates a space where all survivors of abuse and assault can speak up, know that they're not alone, and be affirmed by the tidal wave of other survivors' stories and by abusers being brought to justice. Frankly, the results speak for themselves. And we need to continue highlighting those results, encouraging more survivors to come out of the shadows and bring all perpetrators to justice.

One of those survivors, Rachael Denhollander, will always be a hero to me. Rachael is one of the first women to speak up about the abuse she suffered at the hands of USA Gymnastics team doctor Larry Nassar. Her speaking up opened the way for hundreds of other women to share their stories, including Olympic gold medalists Simone Biles, Aly Raisman and Jordyn Wieber. This phalanx of women stood together, supported one another, and brought their abuser, Nassar, to justice. This is what happens when women draw together and—beyond the distractions of politics and division—focus on what they are truly fighting for. We need to hold them up as examples and should strive to emulate this example in our daily lives. Stand up for your sisters; stand with your sisters.

When I envision leaders who have empowered other women, Rosa Parks immediately comes to mind. Some may not consider Parks's refusal to move from her seat to be an example of standing up and speaking up, but I have always found her simple action to be revolutionary. By doing what was right, not moving from her place on the bus, Parks exemplifies true feminism. And think of all the women who have been empowered or encouraged through Parks's example. I also think about Malala Yousafzai, the Pakistani woman who nearly lost her life for promoting the education of girls. And then there's Oprah

Winfrey, who has created numerous opportunities for women to be educated, to use their voices and tell their stories. To me, these women embody feminism. I may not agree with every detail of their lives but devaluing a woman's impact by niggling over one detail or another undermines authentic feminism and distracts us from its true purpose of bringing women together. We should acknowledge how, even though we may not subscribe to everything that another person says or does, they shouldn't be dismissed or dumped because we may disagree on a few details. This unfortunately seems to happen constantly in our world today; we need to change it.

Feminism has been defined as "the advocacy of women's rights on the basis of the equality of the sexes." But throughout the years, feminism has mutated into so many different issues and elements that we've lost sight of the very root of what we should be fighting for. Some people refuse to even say the word "feminism" because it's become so divisive and politicized. Others use it, but it's come to mean different things to different people. Feminism has been redefined in so many different ways and has become so divisive and politicized, that it's set us back. It's time for us to journey back to our roots and while on that path look at what is actually going on in our society regarding women. We need to listen to every woman as she voices her story, her experience—be it Michelle Williams, Leah Darrow, Rachael Denhollander, or those who have not made the news. We need to recognize the real issues in our society, including women who have been led to believe that they can't have it all. And if they do find it hard to balance it all, we need to create structures to ensure that they have the support that they need. The current discussions overlook the actual root of feminism—women's unmistakable power to transform the world.

Women are resilient, forceful, incredible—but we often overlook those qualities in ourselves or in our sisters. True feminism enables women to recognize their value and their purpose, to bring their power to bear in transforming the world. We should celebrate our uniqueness—our perspectives, our experiences, our relationships—and celebrate such dimensions in the lives of women around us. Sometimes we let our differing perspectives and opinions distract us from what's really at stake and what we're fighting for. Instead, if each of us would celebrate our own and our sisters' uniqueness, a world-changing army would rise up. If women acknowledged their power, their purpose, and their value the world would look a whole lot different.

When my mother was growing up many considered *The Feminine Mystique* to be revolutionary, but she saw the flaws in Friedan's beliefs and in the movement her book sparked. My mom's approach to feminism, which in turn has become mine, is that women deserve to be treated as equal human beings, deserve to be heard and empowered, deserve to "have it all" (but, of course, need to put in the work for it), deserve every opportunity imaginable. But like everyone else, women need to fight for it, and at times we may need to fight harder.

Through our lives and our actions women have the power to change the world; we can do anything we can imagine. There will be roadblocks to bypass and concrete walls to be broken through, but we can be that change if we muster the courage and put in the work. A true feminist reminds, reaffirms, and empowers women so they can recognize and implement their own power, strength, and resilience.

I mentioned before that for me the woman who embodies true feminism is the Blessed Mother—Mary. She did not fear to speak up and to stand up. By her "yes" she empowered and elevated every person who has come after her. Look to Mary for inspiration—in your life as a woman and as a feminist. The Blessed Mother is the original feminist, the ultimate feminist, a beacon for all women.

ⓜ

Chapter 8

"I am not afraid . . .
I was born to do this"

One of my favorite quotes is from Joan Arc: "I am not afraid. . . I was born to do this." The Blessed Mother embodies the same fearlessness. She is the archetype of the incredible women we were created to be. The Blessed Mother was and is a leader. From the time of the apostles to the present day, in cultures throughout the world—Our Lady of Guadalupe in Mexico, Our Lady of Good Health in India, Our Lady of Knock in Ireland, Our Lady of Akita in Japan, too many to count— she is held in high regard as the archetypal Christian, the ultimate example of what it means to be a woman. In every age and culture, the Blessed Mother epitomizes leadership and inspires reverence. Mary's life and choices led the early church and she continues to do the same for every age, every people. Like Mary, women are called to lead through their lives. More than we often realize, women have magnificent power. Who has not witnessed the effect of mothers and other women in their lives? And watching women throughout my life, I would argue:

Women are *the most powerful of God's creatures!*

Women are incredibly resilient. They have a special capacity to grow new life and cultivate and empower others. Every person has the potential to change the world through their lives, but women have a special gift and power. Yet whenever I see one woman competing against another, gossiping about other women, cutting other women down, struggling with imposter syndrome—thinking "I am not worthy"—I realize how important it is that women support one another. I am no stranger to any of this; unfortunately, it's a near-daily struggle. I have always taken the motto "the struggle is real" to heart because it's always been such a big part of my life. I know it's a little kitschy and not on trend, but I still use it and I think it rings true in so many instances in our lives—so don't @ me.

I know women who have come through abuse, human trafficking, addiction, or trauma and have survived. Such women perfectly encapsulate power and resilience. When they rise above whatever has happened to them or whatever they've done—when they rise to empowerment—they raise up and empower those around them. Yet sometimes we women, stifled by shame and pain, thwart our own power.

Ladies, think about the moments when you have held yourself back and stifled what you knew you could do. Think about moments when you had an idea, when you could have taken the initiative, when you had a dream placed on your heart, but you talked yourself out of it or focused on all the reasons that you shouldn't do it. And for everyone else, think about the moments when you have circumvented a woman who wanted to stand up, speak up, or chase her dreams. Think about the moments that you cut a woman down (sisters, we do that to other women all the time) or simply didn't support her (ladies, support your sisters). Day in and day out there are so many instances when women feel like they're standing alone because no one will listen, no one will support them.

Now, I'm not trying to spin about victimhood. In fact, I'm very much against encouraging anyone to feel like a victim or to wallow in "victimhood culture." But a very real discussion needs to happen about women and their power, and how so many things—in the Church, in the culture, in our world—are holding women back from becoming the empowered, world-changing persons we were created to be.

Every woman could tell a story of being held back. Like most women, in office meetings or rooms full of people I myself have been talked over or shushed. I don't dwell on those memories, but such things happen to us—day in and day out. Many hazards that we don't often talk about or dwell on trouble us. After night falls, every woman has had to walk somewhere or drive home by herself, feeling threatened that she might be attacked. Every woman could tell the story of inappropriate comments directed toward them—about their weight, their sexuality, or their appearance. Each and every woman could tell of feeling like she was alone in a silo with no one listening to her voice, her story, or her ideas. Women hold many stories within, but so much of their wisdom is left unheard and unseen. That's why I believe that women need power—and we need to empower ourselves—to be the women we were created to be, and to lead.

Every single day women have such experiences (sometimes men as well). It needs to change. In a world rampant with experiences of being held back, ignored, threatened, criticized, isolated we must choose—am I a victim or am I victorious? I have dealt with many situations where I was talked over or silenced or excluded, but those instances made me stronger. They fueled my passion for speaking up and standing up, for empowering other women and their voices. My encounters with Aunt Alice and Aunt Patricia are examples of being disregarded and having my beliefs dismissed, another element of being hindered. Such life experiences have made me into the woman that I am still becoming. Certainly, they did not have to happen and in many instances, I wish they hadn't. But I chose resilience over suppression, victory over victimhood.

I thought about this when I read Rachael Denhollander's book, *What Is a Girl Worth?* Denhollander was one of the first women to speak up about the abuses of USA Gymnastics team doctor Larry Nassar. Her courage paved the way for more than five hundred other women to come forward; together they brought Nassar to justice. Not only did they achieve justice for themselves, but they stopped

Nassar and others from hurting many other women and girls in years to come.

I've mentioned other women who I have always respected for their willingness to speak up in defense of their sisters. Harriet Tubman escaped slavery to become a leading abolitionist. Her courage led hundreds of other enslaved people to freedom through the Underground Railroad. Rosa Parks stood her ground when she, as a black woman, was told to move. She was arrested. That simple act of courage of refusing to move from her seat ignited a revolution that brought the evils of segregation into the public eye and helped to spark the Civil Rights Movement.

And then, of course, another recent example of a courageous woman is Malala Yousafzai, who defied the Taliban in Pakistan and demanded that girls be allowed to receive an education. A Taliban assassin attempted to kill her, but she survived. Malala's courage to stand up and speak up focused worldwide awareness on the suppression of women and the lack of resources and education opportunities for women and girls. Malala raised awareness of this need and continues to advocate for the education of women and girls around the world.

These are only a few examples of women who by standing up have raised up an army behind them. At moments in our lives we suffer from imposter syndrome, but we need to challenge ourselves to stand up, to rise above such self-judgment because as women we have a unique power to change the world through our lives and to empower others to rise up alongside them.

Joan of Arc's statement, "I am not afraid. . . I was born to do this" embodies what each of us should strive for every single day. We were born for a unique purpose; we should never talk ourselves down or hold ourselves back from acknowledging, like Joan, who we were created to be and what we were created to do.

Growing up, I loved the *Saturday Night Live* skit with Mike Myers and Nicole Kidman playing little kids on the playground. Kidman offers Myers a treat that would make him hyper, but before accepting it he says, "You're the devil!" I often think about that phrase during moments when I hesitate to step onto the path laid before me . . . because I'm insecure, scared, for whatever reason. When we succumb to imposter syndrome, when we hold back from doing something that we feel called to do because we're fearful or unsure, that is the devil. So, when I realize I am drawing back from who I am and what I've been created to do, I say a prayer to Michael the Archangel. If you're not familiar with the story, Michael is the leader of the army of angels who cast Satan and all evil spirits out of heaven. The prayer asks Michael to protect us and to "thrust into hell Satan and all the evil spirits." When negative thoughts surface I'll invoke Michael or say, "Get behind me, Satan. I am not afraid. . . I was born to do this'"

Women have the power to lead. Think of the Blessed Mother, Rosa Parks, Rachael Denhollander, and women like them. Women were created to lead the world toward the good. You may remember from your Sunday school class (or maybe from Jeopardy) that Eve was the first to eat from the Tree of Knowledge and then it was SHE that offered it to Adam, by which they both disobeyed God. When I heard that story as a little kid I could not believe it. "A girl would NEVER do that!" I was shocked that a woman would disobey God (LOL! Now that I'm older and wiser, I know that we all do—unfortunately.). But the bigger takeaway for me, as a little kid and even more so now, was Eve's power. She had the power to lead Adam away from sin or toward it; unfortunately, she chose the latter. And when Mary comes into the picture as the new Eve, with the same power to lead away from sin or toward it, she—thankfully for us—chose the former. This is one of the many reasons why I admire the Blessed Mother and have such an affection for her. She reminds me that even in our darkest moments, our most sinful, our most broken, we can choose to fight for the good, to fight for love. And Mary reminds me that we can always strive to be the women we were created to be—more like Mary than Eve. Mary laid the path for us to be world-changing women for the good.

Above all, women are called to lead and we have the power to do so in new ways—to lead toward the changes we want to see in the world. So own it, embrace it. And when you do, aim to be less Eve and more Mary.

Chapter 9

Singleness and Women without Children

In countless ways and aspects of life, women are called to lead. That call is commonly expressed in two ways: in a career or in family life (or a combination of the two). In reality, however, the variations in women's vocations and how women live their lives is countless. For instance, as I write this book I am thirty-six, never married, and don't have children. By cultural standards I'm "normal," since many are putting off marriage until their late thirties or even forties or fifties, but some may perceive me as a unicorn. In the Catholic community, for instance, I sense that people don't know what to do with me (and others in their thirties or older who are still single). Catholic women (and men) feel a subtle pressure to get married young, and once you're out of your twenties, parishes offer few resources or little support for unmarried individuals, nor for married couples without children. And it seems somewhat the same outside the Catholic world. Most of my friends who do feel part of a community achieve that because they are friends with their kids' friends' parents, or friends with moms from their "Mommy and Me" classes. Rarely does a day go by when I'm not asked if I'm married or if I have kids; my married friends who have no children are often asked if they have kids.

We need not be defined by our relationship status, our family life, our kids (or our lack thereof). Those things are a part of life, but not what defines it. But adults feel such pressure to focus on marriage and children. I want to address that, and this book is a start. In this chapter, I'll share my experiences as a single woman in the world and in the church, with a focus on another similar cohort of people who are often forgotten about and marginalized—those who have no children, due to infertility or for other reasons.

Let's talk about dating first because, well, I've got some juicy stories for you. We'll see what life brings between now, as I write this, and when this book gets published, but no matter what happens, even if I'm still single, I love my life and I know that I'm exactly where I am supposed to be. At times I struggle inside because I would love to be married and have a family, but I've learned to embrace who I am and where I am at this stage (and at every stage) in my life. And as much as I would love to share this life with someone, I am confident that I'm exactly where I'm supposed to be, doing exactly what I was always meant to be doing. This is but one chapter in my life—a chapter that could last my whole life, but I'm confident that God wants to fulfill the desires of each person's heart. While I've been single much longer than I ever imagined, I know that God is working, and no matter what happens I'm learning to embrace each chapter and to seize the moments—including singleness—that each chapter includes.

For me, singlehood could last the rest of my days. I recognize that, but I've built up a life that I'd be happy with, whether I marry or stay single. I also recognize that I'm never, ever, actually alone. I have a great family, great friends, hobbies, community, and a very full life—even if I don't have one particular person, day in and day out, to share it with.

When I was just a girl, I remember thinking my mom was "old" when she got married at thirty-four. Now thirty-four seems young. When I was younger, I imagined that I would be married by twenty-five and have a whole brood of kids—I told folks that I wanted to have a dozen. That obviously hasn't happened, but I'm still holding out for the possibility of a bunch. . . especially if I have a few biological children and do foster care and adopt a few. My dream isn't outside the realm of possibility.

When I was younger I didn't date a lot. My parents wouldn't allow me until I turned sixteen, but I ended up not dating until I was eighteen. I have always been very intentional in how I live my life and I look at relationships in the same way. From the moment I began wearing my first chastity ring at sixteen, I wanted to be intentional in who and how I dated. When I was eighteen, my first experience with dating seemed perfect. I met a guy on one of the summer-long mission trips I participated in and I fell head over heels.

I remember thinking how easy dating was. I believed that I had met "my person," that we'd date throughout college, get married after we graduated, and live happily ever after. All summer we read chastity books together and prayed the rosary together, and wow . . . in my mind, it was perfect! But you know what they say about people who meet on mission trips—you get the "pilgrimage high," then things crash and burn when you come back into the real world. And that's exactly what happened. It didn't work out for us, but a few months later the guy did meet his future wife, is now married, and they have a bunch of kids.

Funny story: almost immediately after dating me every guy either has met his wife or become a priest. LOL. So, I often joke that my vocation is helping men find their vocations. None of these relationships were meant to develop and obviously God has other plans both for me and for these guys. But, come on God, at some point some guy's gotta help me find my vocation. Come on, God, help a sista out!

I've never been overly concerned and always feel that each person I date leads me to the next. I've always seen these temporary relationships as "breadcrumbs" leading me toward the person I'm really supposed to end up with, or as "puzzle pieces" that will come together to reveal the full picture of my life. Even at thirty-six, I still believe that.

From my eighteen-year-old boyfriend to today, my life has felt like "The Catholic Bachelorette" on a rollercoaster. I've been on countless dates, most of them with really good guys. Each one taught me something important about myself—who I am, what I need, and what I want. When I was younger, I thought that you shouldn't date a lot, maybe a byproduct of Joshua Harris, but I have come to believe that once you're at an age where it makes sense (maybe older than sixteen), dating can be a good thing because you learn how to interact with others and it helps you figure out exactly what you want and need.

I've dated many different types, and each guy has had negatives and positives; but above all I've learned something from every one of them. Every relationship has been a lesson in life and love. We can learn from every interaction—even in prospective relationships. Even before going on a date with me, I've had guys do an internet search about me, which could be a good thing or a bad thing. On the one hand, it's refreshing because you can learn a lot about me through things I've written about and done; but on the other hand, we all want to be authentically known and I want the guy I end up with to know me for who I truly am. I want someone to get to know me, not just "cram" like I'm an exam to take and get over with. I've also had guys that say in their online profiles (or in life) that they want a woman with a "fearless heart," but what they really want is a plaid jumper-wearing, Latin-Mass-attending baby mama who has no interests or aspirations beyond being a wife and mother. Spoiler alert for any guys who may be reading this: All women have hobbies, interests, and things that bring her joy in addition to being a wife and mother, or whatever her vocation may be. And these personal dimensions should be encouraged and embraced. As with my own mother, we are better women and better wives and mothers for having our own interests, careers, hobbies, or pursuits.

As I've gotten older, dating has gotten more complicated. I see two main categories of men and women in the dating market—not the sole categories, but the main ones. They are: 1) people of faith with very specific and for the most part unrealistic expectations for a marriage partner —e.g., a virginal saint with no dreams or aspirations, solely dedicated to his or her spouse and family, willing to let the spouse go off playing golf, going to sporting events, or do whatever else while he or she happily sits at home doing laundry, cooking, and tending the house and children. Those who are looking for a spouse like that are so zero-focused on their own desires that they don't want to make any changes or sacrifices; they want someone who simply gets in line and fits into the crevices of their life. And 2) men or women who have lived "worldly" lives, but now want a calmer, happier life and are striving to be stable partners; they want to find someone for a serious relationship. Usually such people haven't met many "good guys" or "good girls," so they struggle at times to believe that such possible partners exist. They've spent a lot of time chasing after people that weren't good for them.

In all honesty, I myself have wavered between these two categories. Sometimes I've had unrealistic expectations for the person that I'm looking for, other times I feel like I'm finally in a place where I'm ready for something serious and ready to "do life" with someone. However, we can hold ourselves back from happiness while Satan spins doubt in our minds whether there is a perfect person out there for us or that the perfect person for us isn't quite perfect enough. In reality, perfect doesn't exist—unless you're Jesus. But I do believe that our journey is "perfect" for us and if there is a "perfect" person for us in our unique life journey, God has one in mind.

Full disclosure: I don't have anything figured out and I don't claim to. I can only share my own experience. I'm not perfect and I don't claim to be, but like you, I'm striving to live life in the best way I can.

My dad has always said that if you want to get married and have a family you need to treat dating like a job and put in the same effort that you do with your career, which can be exhausting. And he's right. Throughout every experience—both good and bad—I've learned a great deal from each guy that I've dated and vice versa (I hope!). Two guys that I've dated recently were polar opposites, but each made me see things I didn't realize about myself and have helped me prepare for a lifelong commitment with the one I'm meant to marry.

Two years ago, a close friend set me up with the brother of one of her other friends. For months it seemed to be a great match, but then quickly began to dissipate. There are two sides to every story, but I felt (and still do) that our relationship started unraveling when I shared that I was saving sex for marriage. This guy came from a "good Catholic family" and in many ways was a "good Catholic man," but it became very clear that for him a dating relationship had to include sex. And my stance seemed to be a hurdle he could never really get over. I don't blame him because we live in a culture that has tried to convince us that sex and "hooking up" is an essential part of every romantic relationship. I definitely have gone countercultural on that. This is not to say that sex isn't integral to our lives and relationships, but I've always believed that it should be rightly ordered and to me, there is a distinct right place for sex—in marriage. Most frustrating was that he never really seemed to try to understand my decision, never asked any questions. It felt like he tried to ignore it or hoped that one day, out of the blue, I would tell him that my mind had changed. I realized that he hadn't lived his life in the same way as I had, and I didn't judge him for it, but I felt like he judged me and my decision frustrated him.

Our biggest hurdle, though, was that he had his "bachelor life" and wanted a woman he could cram into whatever cracks of time he had available after he did all the things he wanted. I loved him, but I always felt like I was second or third to everything— sports, his job, his family, his friends. I'm pretty independent and always have things going on, hobbies and projects I'm working on, so I didn't feel totally abandoned but I never felt like a priority for him, which is a major problem in a relationship. I share this story because no person should ever feel like only an afterthought. I brought it up on numerous occasions throughout our relationship of almost a year, but it became clear that nothing was going to change, and we were never going to be a good fit. So things didn't work out.

A few months later, I was ready to get back into the game—I mean, I'm well into my thirties and if I'm serious about finding a partner and getting married, I have to continue putting myself out there. Remembering what my dad said about treating dating like a job, I got on a couple of dating apps. I met a guy and on our first date, there was a connection. We ended up dating a few months and a great relationship seemed to be developing, but in the end we weren't the right fit for each other. This guy helped me heal a lot of the wounds inflicted by the previous person I dated, was really supportive of everything I was doing, and always prioritized us and our relationship. But he wasn't "the one." Our breakup turned out to be a really healing and beautiful experience that showed me—unlike what transpired in my previous relationships—that adults can handle things in better ways than ghosting, anger, or worse. I share this to note how dating and relationships always should be leading and guiding us to grow. Every person we meet, encounter, or date can lead us to who we're supposed to be with and who we're meant to become. Not having a fiancé or husband suggests that I may not be an expert on dating and relationships, but my experience does confirm that the most perfect relationship(s) should lead us to love others better and to love better ourselves and who we were created to be.

Dating has gotten more and more complicated and difficult for me, not just because I'm getting older, but also because of how our world and our culture has continued to evolve. One decision that I've made and upheld every single day has definitely helped me lessen the complicated nature of relationships—my commitment to chastity. I'm not saying that chastity will "solve" all issues in relationships. If that were the case, I'd still be in one of my previous relationships. But my consistent decision to save sex for marriage has allowed me to see every relationship through clearer eyes and has protected and saved me from bad situations. When I was younger, I used to expect that guys should and would share the same beliefs as I had, but as I've gotten older and gotten to know so many guys and learned more about their journey, I've concluded that whoever I end up with doesn't have to have lived his life in the same way as I have. But the non-negotiable is they must R-E-S-P-E-C-T my decisions and how I've chosen to live my life. This is all to say that you don't have to live your life like I have, but if I could share one piece of advice it would be this: RESPECT must be non-negotiable.

Real talk: If you EVER feel pressured or feel that someone is pushing your boundaries, walk . . . no, RUN . . . run away as fast as you possibly can! A person who doesn't respect your boundaries or your choices does not deserve another moment of your time. Singlehood days can be lonely and sometimes painful; I feel that pain regularly. But I remain steadfast in my confidence that God is working. When the time is right and the right person comes into my life I'll be ready for marriage and a family!

The greatest gifts of my singlehood days have been relationships and friendships with my sisters, my gal pals. Many of my friends and I are going through the same thing, aching for marriage and family, but not yet having met the right person. But not having spouses and children has allowed us the freedom to dedicate more time to family and friends. Religious sisters, or others who are unmarried and living out the single life, also have a similar capacity to serve and to help others. My married friends who don't have children—due to infertility or other reasons—also have had similar opportunities. Many of my married friends without children, because they don't have kids, have been able to be there for me and many of our other friends. This is not to make light of their struggles and pain, but sometimes God allows these different chapters of whatever we're experiencing so we can be there for others. In a similar vein, those who are divorced, widowed, or annulled—both women and men whose dating and relationship experiences are different than mine—can share their particular experience with others who are facing similar circumstances.

I bring up these different categories because none of us fit into the status quo nor into the church or the culture" boxes" whereby every woman is seen as a "mom" or a "single." Those categories do not match the demographics. When I think about all of this and about Betty Friedan and her followers in the "women's rights" movement, I can't help but think that their advocacy didn't change all that many things for women. Of course, some women indeed do "have-it-all"—a career, hobbies, husband, and children. But they are an exception. Overall, women are judged—especially according to surface impressions—mainly by their relational status (single or married, with or without kids). That's wrong.

Women have more dimensions than whether they are single or married, whether they have children or not. Every woman—married or single, with children or without—is an integral person, a mother of sorts to many people throughout her life. Each woman has unique interests, facets, and capabilities; each is authentic in her own way. Much still needs to be done in the world and in the church to acknowledge each woman's unique purpose. Her journey matters and has value; her voice and her life matter.

Chapter 10

Women Leaders in the Church... and in the World

A few months ago, I joined a panel with two married women and a nun for an online discussion for young Catholics about faith and life. We talked about relationships, women we admired, our personal struggles, our prayer life, and more. At one point, the moderator asked a question about motherhood. The second that the question came up I knew that the panel would beeline past me. I didn't take it personally at all. This wasn't my first rodeo; I know how people in the church often work.

Sure enough, the married women (and the nun) took ownership of the motherhood question and then the moderator quickly moved onto the next question without coming to me. Again, I didn't take it personally; I don't think they were trying to single me out. People may think that they're being helpful by avoiding the awkwardness of calling attention to motherhood with a woman who is single and childless. In fact, however, there's something beautiful about giving such women the opportunity to speak on motherhood, especially since no matter what our personal story is, motherhood is an integral part of womanhood. And you don't have to have children to be a mother or mother figure to others.

As I listened to the next question, about competition and how we should support other women around us instead of competing with them, something was brewing within me. When I'm frustrated or upset, I tend to mull over whatever is gnawing at me inside, come up with my response, and then come out swinging. As they say, don't mess with an Irish woman. So, I thought through it, formulated a response, and when it was my turn to speak again I was ready with a curveball.

The conversation had turned to women and competition—certainly an important topic—and I was ready. I started off by saying that I would address the question about competition, but first I wanted to pivot back to the topic of motherhood.

All women, whether they have a spouse or not, whether they have children or not, are spiritual mothers. For all women, whether biological mothers or not, motherhood is an integral part of womanhood. Every woman's life includes children—nieces and nephews, cousins, the children of our friends, neighborhood kids, and more—for whom we have the responsibility to be present. All women not only have a responsibility to be a part of these children's lives, but we also hold a unique ability to connect with them, to be "mothers" and mentors to all children in our lives. And the culture—especially church culture—needs to highlight and encourage such motherhood. That's what I told the online forum.

There's a good reason why the Catholic Church often gets attacked for being "anti-woman" or for not recognizing women's integral role. Pictures of the Blessed Mother and female saints are plastered all over our churches, but panel discussions at faith conferences generally include very few women. When you look at the structure and staff of churches—although some significant strides have been made—it's still rare to see women in the lineup. That being said, at its core Catholicism has the most authentic and fullest understanding of women's value in the church and in the world. The Catholic Church recognizes the dignity and power of women but needs to improve how it integrates those qualities in its everyday life.

Just as Mary is a mother to all of us, all women should emulate her as a mother-figure for the children in their lives. My experience on the panel reflects the issues regarding women and the church. Although they may not have given birth, single women and married women without children are still "mothers" whose womanhood should be recognized and esteemed. The Catholic Church acknowledges the greatness of Mary's motherhood, as it should, but the connection I feel to her has to do with who she was as a woman—not just who she was as a mother. And that's how the culture and the church should recognize all women—for their womanhood—including those of us who are single. Whether our motherhood is spiritual or biological, above all else we are women. Catholics recognize Mary's power as we look to her for intercession and guidance, and as an example of resilience and empowerment. I've always loved the Blessed Mother, and as I've gotten older my devotion and love has only gotten stronger. Visiting many of Mary's apparition sites—Fatima, Lourdes, Guadalupe, Knock, and Medjugorje—has made me appreciate one woman's power to transform the world. Mary is an awe-inspiring example of womanhood and motherhood, and like her every woman, whether a biological mother or not, exemplifies womanhood and motherhood. Along their life journey women have a unique feminine power to encounter others and to empathize and heal in ways that men cannot. Men have their own gifts, talents, and powers, but it's important to foreground the uniqueness of women, their lives, and their impact on the world.

Many Catholics look to certain individuals as the embodiment of womanhood: Edith Stein, Catherine of Siena, Joan of Arc, Therese of Lisieux, and Mother Teresa served the church, transformed the world through their lives, and empowered others. But in my mind the Blessed Mother will always be the GOAT. At the Wedding at Cana, when she told him about the wine having run out, Mary suggested that Jesus perform a miracle. That's gotta take some grit to tell the son of God what you want him to do! But truly, what son wouldn't do something generous when his mother asks that of him? Which is also why we ask

Mary to pray for us—to bring our intentions to her son. I admire other women in the church and in the world, but the Blessed Mother truly embodies feminism and womanhood. I also admire (and saw in person at World Youth Day 2002!) a certain individual in the church with a strong devotion to the Blessed Mother who understood and recognized women's awesome value and power to transform the world: John Paul II.

In his encyclical *Redemptoris Mater* John Paul II wrote:

> It can thus be said that women, by looking to Mary, find in her the secret of living their femininity with dignity and of achieving their own true advancement. In the light of Mary, the Church sees in the face of women the reflection of a beauty which mirrors the loftiest sentiments of which the human heart is capable: the self-offering totality of love; the strength that is capable of bearing the greatest sorrows; limitless fidelity and tireless devotion to work; the ability to combine penetrating intuition with words of support and encouragement. (46)

By the light of Mary, women illuminate what the human heart is capable of, truly and fully. I love that thought from the encyclical. This is not to diminish or disregard men, but women do bring to light what humans are truly meant to be. And Mary is the perfect example, a woman who we should all emulate.

In his "Letter to Women," John Paul II discusses women's special, God-given gift to see others with their hearts, their ability to reveal the greatness of others and the beauty of humanity. He writes:

> Perhaps more than men, women acknowledge the person, because they see persons with their hearts. They see them independently of various ideological or political systems. They see others in their greatness and limitations; they try to go out to them and help them. In this way the basic plan of the Creator takes flesh in the history of humanity and there is constantly revealed, in the variety of vocations, that beauty— not merely physical, but above all spiritual—which God bestowed from the very beginning on all, and in a particular way on women. (12)

Women are not superior to men, but different. Women may not realize their own power, their unique gifts and talents, who and what they were created to be and to do—to encounter others and raise them up in a special way. And when women recognize and exemplify this, the world looks much different, and better. Through their lives women have the power to change the world; we need to believe that and embrace that. And the church and the world are better when women's gifts are recognized and elevated.

His "Letter to Women" details women's power to change the world:

> Women will increasingly play a part in the solution of the serious problems of the future: leisure time, the quality of life, migration, social services, euthanasia, drugs, health care, the ecology, etc.

In all these areas a greater presence of women in society will prove most valuable, for it will help to manifest the contradictions present when society is organized solely according to the criteria of efficiency and productivity, and it will force systems to be redesigned in a way which favors the processes of humanization which mark the "civilization of love." (4)

Women can transform the world by building up a civilization of love. They hold the solutions to the world's many serious problems, today and in the future. Women lead the charge to end homelessness, human trafficking, and other evils in our world. But women must recognize the power they hold and own it. The church has a special responsibility to set an example in elevating women and their voices. We, as a society and as a church, should heed women's voices, listen to their stories, and experiences; support women's dreams and ideas; promote their empowerment. Women don't need special treatment, but in the culture and the church women have not yet been elevated as they ought to be. And, as women, we must do a better job supporting and raising up our sisters, the women around us.

Prior to the 1960's, reflecting the culture of the time, the Catholic Church reflected a male bias. When families went to Mass, the man typically took the lead and the woman made sure that the kids were clean and ready. At church, women would cover their heads with a veil or—and as comical as it might seem now, even a tissue if they didn't have a mantilla handy—and were expected to be meek, mild, and subdued. Since those days, the church has made leaps forward by elevating women to positions of leadership, but more needs to be done. The same is true in mainstream culture. I get frustrated when I scan a list of corporate boards of directors or church committees and see few women (or none!). Or at conferences—be they Evangelical or Catholic or secular—I find that women are lacking big time in the lineup. Women don't need quotas, but every aspect of the world could do better in opening up spaces for women's voices and perspectives. As John Paul II wrote, women's "ability to combine penetrating intuition with words of support and encouragement" is integral to "the processes of humanization which mark the 'civilization of love.'" Society owes it to itself for women to be represented in every aspect.

Some in the church still expect women to be meek, calm, and collected as the Blessed Mother is often presented. But that's a false image. The real Mary is not quiet. She's a revolutionary. She's fierce and strong. Recently a guy I had met through a Catholic dating app wrote that he wanted a woman with a "fierce heart." When we met, though, he shared that he was looking for someone mild-mannered as he perceived the Blessed Mother to be, someone who wanted to stay home and raise a family. That guy's view reflects the way many in the church see the Blessed Virgin, but that is hardly how I see her. "A fierce heart," yes . . . but not meek in a conventional sense. Jesus' beatitude, "the meek shall inherit the earth," is misunderstood to mean that the meek are subservient and quiet. But the Greek word that has been translated as "meek," πράος, is also used to describe a horse that has been «broken" for saddle riding. That horse may be obedient to its rider, but still has its strength and passion. Strength and passion! That's how I see Mary. Mary obeyed God, yes, but was a warrior; that's what God has instilled within every woman. I wish church people would do a better job of highlighting Mary's strength and passion and conveying that. Thankfully, John Paul II and others really "got it," but their writings aren't highlighted enough.

Throughout his writings John Paul II emphasizes that, like the Blessed Mother, women have a unique power to transform the world; he calls for women to recognize their own value, their own purpose, and their own power, and encourages others to do the same. Women, whatever their vocation or status in life, have a unique purpose and power to heal the world's wounds. Every woman. In our daily life, let's work harder to elevate women and their voices, and let this female revolution start to change the world.

Chapter 11

Let Your Life Set the World Ablaze

"If you are what you should be, you will set the whole world ablaze." I've always loved this quote; it ought to be tattooed on every heart. We were created for a purpose, a unique mission—to leave a singular imprint on this world that no one else can. Like our fingerprints, each of us is unique. If we truly believed that and lived so as to communicate that it's true, our lives would look a whole lot different. And our world would look a whole lot different if every one of us recognized and embraced our singular purpose.

When I was fifteen a single event rocked my entire family's life, as well as mine—my grandfather's suicide. I wasn't close to him, mainly because he was not a good person; he had tormented many people's lives. My parents made it a point not to allow us to be alone with him (for very, very good reasons). The tremendous harm and pain he caused still lingers in the lives of many he left behind. I too carry his suicide with me every day. That one action of his opened my eyes in a new way to how fragile human life is. It also made me see myself as a survivor.

Looking back at his life I recall how many times my grandfather had the choice to do good or to do bad, to hurt or to heal. Unfortunately, even with his last breath he chose to cause injury and pain. It's been more than twenty years since my dad found his dead body, and to this day I don't know how to process what it must have felt like to have a father who had wounded so many throughout his life, then to recognize that even in his last moment he chose to cause pain and suffering. We've found healing, but the wounds he caused still run deep throughout the family. I often think of my grandfather when I consider how my own everyday choices can sow darkness or shed light.

I love Disney and the *Star Wars* franchise . . . I grew up watching all the movies. One of my favorite aspects is its clear depiction of light and darkness, and "the force." *Star Wars* let us mark how people can choose the light—the good—or the "dark side." That dichotomy represents our lives—the power of sin and darkness, but also the light and strength we hold to heal the world and transform it for good.

Earlier, I singled out women's power to change the world and to heal, but every person holds the power to change the world and to heal others. Every single day we need to recognize our power and choose to use it. We must summon our courage and cultivate our gifts and talents; we must stand in the place we were created for. Joan of Arc said, "I am not afraid. . . I was born to do this." You were created for greatness, but you must make a choice—you must choose light over darkness. We were created in love and for love, but abuse, pain, suffering, and other darknesses can overwhelm lives created for love, created to be love in the world. This is not to justify evil, but just as in my grandfather's life and in *Star Wars*, some let darkness overtake them.

On the flipside, though, if you are what you were created to be, what you're meant to be, you'll help heal the world's brokenness; your life will change the world; you'll set the whole world ablaze.

There are so many problems in the world, so much pain and suffering. We see them every single day; often they touch us personally. Maybe we ourselves have caused some of that pain and suffering. Things have caused us pain or still do, things we've done that we're not proud of. Maybe we were raised in an abusive household and have passed that abuse on to others, or maybe we were raised without boundaries and good values, so we have lived a life without boundaries and morals. No matter what has happened to us or what we've done, we can always hope. My parents grew up in abusive and unstable homes but chose to rise above it (processing it all and finding healing, of course) and they chose to stop the cycle of abuse. As we grew up my sisters and brother and I knew what my parents had experienced, and we know that the cycle of abuse stopped with them. What healing they generated by raising us in a loving, warm, safe home! Just as with so many things in our lives, we have the power to choose good, to weave goodness and love, to heal the past, the present, and the future.

A quote often attributed to Maya Angelou says, "As soon as healing takes place, go out and heal somebody else." We must allow healing, let our brokenness and the wounds that we carry around with us be healed, and then we will have the power to heal the world. I often mention things that I went through in my own life and how, in a way, I'm glad I went through what I did. Because of what we have experienced, what we have gone through, we may be able to help someone else. This is not to say that bad things should happen; I wish bad things never happened. Unfortunately, they sometimes do, but if we let ourselves be healed after such experiences, we can use that experience to help someone else. This is the power of therapy, but above all for me the power of the Sacrament of Reconciliation. Sometimes we need to work through something or talk through something to find perspective or healing. There is deep healing to be received from the sacraments, a healing that I've experienced.

When I was in college, my friend Emily and I took a ten-day trip around Europe. Sounds fun, right? It was awesome—one of the craziest, most life-changing experiences that's happened to me. We were studying abroad in Austria for a semester, and during our Easter break we decided to check off as many bucket list sights and cities as we could. This was before smartphones, so if we got into trouble we had no way to call friends or family. At times it was really scary. We got on a wrong train, got kicked off another train in the middle of nowhere, fell asleep and woke up in an empty carriage parked in a train yard, got stranded in the middle of nowhere France because the last train had left. That night we ended up wandering the streets until, thankfully, we stumbled upon a safe place to sleep. I could tell many stories of being in crazy and terrible situations, but thanks to God or our guardian angels or whoever makes miracles happen everything worked out. I still don't know how we survived or how amid the craziness we didn't have breakdowns. But many beautiful things also happened throughout this ten-day journey.

We ended up in places we never anticipated, met people we never would've met, and had experiences that never would have happened. We saw the leaning tower of Pisa (Italy) and Sacré-Cœur (Paris), but one of the most powerful, healing experiences of that trip—honestly, of my life—was Lourdes, where at a grotto the Blessed Mother appeared to Bernadette and healing water began to flow from the stone grotto. We wanted to "stop by" and see the apparition site, but we didn't intend to stay for long. But once we got there, we felt a deep pull to stay.

On the recommendation of some college friends who we happened to run into there at random, we decided to go to the baths. Our Lady instructed Bernadette to "drink at the spring and bathe in it," and since 1858 millions of pilgrims have travelled to Lourdes to do just that. Down through the years, there are said to have been many healings. So, we decided to wait in line and check out the holy and miraculous waters. I don't think I really knew what to expect—

actually I had no idea! And I'm glad I didn't because had I known that you would have to take off your clothes in front of a group of people, get wrapped in a sheet, then get dunked into a bathtub full of freezing holy water, I probably wouldn't have done it.

Before lining up for the baths I went to confession and afterwards felt a tremendous calm. It was as if an ocean wave of peace had broken over me. Usually I've felt peace after confession (except for a few bad experiences when the priest yelled at me or scolded me unnecessarily—but all of us Catholics can commiserate . . . LOL . . . we've all had those experiences!), but never such a WAVE of PEACE. It was so powerful that it nearly brought me to tears—tears of comfort and joy. After confession, I joined the line for the baths. When I finally got to the door, I was shuffled inside behind a line of hanging sheets and quickly some nuns started stripping off my clothes. Right away they wrapped me in one of those sheets, so I didn't feel exposed at all. And then I was shuffled past a few more hanging veils into a little "cubicle" with a bathtub filled with holy Lourdes water from the grotto. Holding my hands, the nuns helped me into the bath, the sheet still wrapped tight around me. They said, "Bring your intentions, everything you have, into the waters with you. . ." Then, "On the count of three, we're going to plunge you into the water . . . one . . . two . . . three. . ." A flood of emotions swept through me. Recalling that moment still summons up powerful feelings. This wave rushing over me was even more intense than the one after my confession.

It was healing, liberating—honestly, it was a moment of wonder, awe, and serenity, one of the greatest I have ever felt.

This story shows the courage it can often take to find peace and healing. But once we muster the courage—much like entering the baths without really knowing what to expect—we find healing and in turn, our healing can resound through our world and empower and heal others. The Blessed Mother brought healing to Bernadette and so many others through the waters of Lourdes. Just so, we can bring a glimmer of light and healing to those around us, to those throughout the world.

The world is infected, it's sick in many ways, probably because its people are infected and sick. We share in this malady, that's for sure, but because we all share the same sickness we all can take part in the healing. It's the people in the church who cause the problems in the church and the same applies to the world. We are the problems, but we also can be the solution to all the issues we see in our church and our world. Division, strife, and brokenness permeate every aspect of our culture worldwide, and many of these illnesses can be laid at our own feet—every one of us. But if we recognize that we are a part of the problem and allow ourselves to be healed, we can be a part of the solution; we can bring healing and peace to those around us and to the world. The world is segregated, stressed, and separated but—as the popular saying goes—»we're stronger together." If we really want to bring wholeness to the fragmentation we see in the world, we need to let healing come to ourselves first, then let peace and healing come to those around us, and so set off a domino effect throughout the world.

To reiterate, John Paul II, channeling Catherine of Siena said, "If you are what you should be, you will set the whole world ablaze." Through your life you have the power to set the whole world ablaze. You have the power to light up the dark and so let healing come to those around you and to the world. First, though, each of us must find healing, peace, and come to know who we were created to be.

Chapter 12

Lessons to Live By–Your Legacy

Just as my life has been a journey, so is writing this book. It took me a while to figure out how I wanted to end this journey with you but—like my life—it is still being written. And just the same, your life is still being written too. I am sitting here, a thirty-six-year-old woman who's saving sex for marriage, who's been through a lot and accomplished a lot, but I know that I'm just getting started. And I know you are too.

Quite often I think about "legacy," especially working in media and PR. The news cycle goes so fast, yet it's also so permanent. With social media and with everything being on record and online, anything that's put out into the universe—be it good or bad—never really goes away. It thus becomes a part of someone's "legacy." In our own lives we need to place more emphasis on legacy; we should all think about and reflect regularly: "What is the legacy I want to leave behind?" As you know, I'm Irish, so growing up I went to tons of funerals. We still rarely miss one. Not just because we have a massive family and older folks are always passing away, but also because my parents believed that it was important to pay our respects to a life that had been lived and to celebrate it. The best part about Irish funerals is how they put celebration into practice; after the funeral usually there's a big party at a local pub or at someone's house. So funerals have never been scary to me; actually, they've always been a space for healing and reflection. And just like this book and our legacies, for the person who passed it's not an end, but a continuing journey beyond this world. I believe in Heaven, and I believe that each person's life continues after this journey through life.

Considering how to end this book, I thought I would wrap it up with some thoughts on legacy and some lessons that I've learned throughout my life. Perhaps they can be a guide when you're thinking about your own life and the legacy that you want to leave.

If I could leave the world one message, it would be that every single person has the power to change the world through their life. Every person's life is a journey, a process, an adventure, and no one's journey is the same. Each one of us was created in love and for love. Each of us is as unique as our fingerprints and each of us has been created for a unique purpose. There is not a single other person that can be what you were created to be for the world and in the world. The world needs you and your life to fulfill the plan for your life in our world—be it God's, or the plan of whoever or whatever you believe in.

Life is an adventure. We should never stop growing, learning, and evolving. Life is a book being written about what we have done, what we have accomplished, and the legacy that we will leave behind. Every moment, every day, every conversation, every relationship, every person we encounter is a part of that story.

Growing up, I regularly heard stories about Blessed Solanus Casey. My grandparents would take me down to Detroit, where he's buried, for healing—of my eczema and for our family. When my great-grandfather was suffering from ALS, Fr. Solanus visited him and his family on numerous occasions. While he wasn't healed—he ended up passing away from the disease—my grandfather, who was sixteen when great-grandfather died, always said that Fr. Solanus brought hope and peace to the family, even amid the suffering. One remarkable thing about Fr. Solanus was that he always carried a little notebook in which he would write down the name of every single person he came in contact with—every person he met, spoke with, prayed with, or ran into. He wrote down every name, things to be prayed for, and little notes for himself. Now that he's passed, those notebooks are on display at the Solanus Casey Center in Detroit. I think about those books often. My great-grandfather's name is in there somewhere, I'm sure, and one day I'd love to see where Fr. Solanus wrote it down and what he wrote. I bring this up because when I think about those notebooks, I think about legacy.

Every person we encounter—be it someone we have dated or become friends with (for a long time or only briefly), family members (our run-ins, debates, or other encounters), acquaintances, everyone—every person, every moment—are all in the notebooks of our lives. In many ways, this book is one of the notebooks where I've written down the people, moments, puzzle pieces of my life. I want to encourage you to think about your life in this way. What experiences—good or bad—are a part of your life story and your legacy? Which people would you write down on the lines of your notebook? What stories? Who are the main characters? Which friends and family members have supported you through thick and thin? Who has harassed you for what you believe? Who told you that you've changed? These are all pieces of your story, parts of your legacy.

And the best part: we can keep writing our stories until our very last breath. As my grandfather Francis said on his deathbed, "I'm still a work in progress." And who knows, maybe our legacy will go on being written after our funeral party is over.

I don't claim to have anything figured out, but throughout my brief life journey I have learned a few things. So I thought I would end by sharing some life lessons that have helped me and still help me as I continue my journey. Here are some of my favorite mantras, life lessons, or things to live by:

Be Not Afraid.

As John Paul II—and you know I love our boy JP2—is often quoted as saying, "I plead with you—never, ever give up on hope, never doubt, never tire, and never become discouraged. **Be not afraid**." Whatever you are ever going through, whatever you're struggling with, whatever path is before you, whatever you experience that might bring uncertainty, anxiety, stress, or fear—be not afraid! At some moments I've had to dig down, deep into my heart and soul, to unearth the courage and strength to overcome my fear and uncertainty. And I always remind myself that God is walking with me, just as he's walking with you. So, be not afraid.

Encounter people on their journey . . . Walk with them.

"Encounter" is a beautiful word that I've come to know, love, and live out in my daily life. As you know by now, I have very strong convictions, and I recognize that most other people in the world have very strong convictions too. But I always seek to "encounter" the person sitting or standing before me, not jump to conclusions about who they are or what they believe, love them for who they are as a fellow human. Sometimes that can be a struggle, especially in dealing with a "negative Nancy" or someone who is just being a pain in the rear. But I remind myself that I don't know what other people are going through in their lives or what they've gone through. So, we need to give each other grace so we can encounter the person before us. Pope Francis says, "Whenever we encounter another person in love, we learn something new about God." I would venture to say that through our encounters with other people, we also learn something new about ourselves—and who we were created to be.

Know what you believe and why you believe it.

This one is pretty straightforward. Don't be afraid to say, "I don't know." I've always loved conversations between people with whom I disagree and those who disagree with me. There have been humbling moments when I got crushed in a discussion or a debate or simply had to say, "I don't know." But overall, I've always known what I believed and why I believe what I believe and have stood strong. It can be difficult to speak up, but being convicted, knowing why we believe what we believe makes speaking up easier. In "Stride toward Freedom," Martin Luther King Jr. said, "The greatest tragedy . . .was not the strident clamor of the bad people, but the appalling silence of the good people." Never be silent in the face of injustice or other matters that need you and your voice. Know what you believe and why you believe it. . . and use your voice.

Use your voice. You will empower others to use their voice.

As the popular saying goes, "Empowered women empower women." I referred to those empowered women earlier in this book. As much as I love that phrase, I would take it a step further to say: Empowered people empower people. I think about Rachael Denhollander, who spoke up against Larry Nassar and raised up an army to bring him to justice. Or Rosa Parks who said "No" and elevated other voices, lives, and stories. So many stories come to mind, so many I could share, but whenever someone speaks up it gives others courage and empowers them to speak. So, use your voice and you will empower others to use their voices too.

Be open.

We're all on our own journey. We bring our own opinions and experiences to the table, but we should never confine our vision to ourselves. We should always be open, always searching for truth. Be humble and recognize that you don't know everything. Listen to others. Be open to other perspectives and further information. No one is perfect. . . recognize that. We should keep our lives and our beliefs open to learning, growing, and evolving. Of course, some things indeed are black and white; truth is truth. Stay open but recognize that on some things we may never change our minds. Humility and openness can open our lives and our hearts in new ways, and our openness and humility can have the same effect on others. So always be humble and open.

Pray

Pray. Pray. "Pray without ceasing" (1 Thessalonians 5:17). In many instances we don't know where to go or what to do, moments in life when we feel absolutely helpless. In those moments I always find myself crying out to God, "Why?" or "Why me?" or "What am I supposed to do?" But throughout each and every day I pray more and more . . . not just at moments when I feel faint or lost or broken. I talk to God like I do to a friend. If you live with roommates or family, that can be awkward . . . LOL . . . especially when they see or hear you talking to the clouds. Ha ha! But we need to change how we think; we need to free ourselves to converse with God, day in and day out. One of my favorite things is to turn the music up loud while driving and just talk to God, or sometimes even talk at God. God's a good listener; God loves to hear from us. So, let God hear from you every day. You may not be in a prayerful position, holding your Bible . . . you may be speaking through a Mumford and Sons song or just walking through your neighborhood. Talk to God. Pray without ceasing.

Give God pep talks.

Recently I've come to love giving God pep talks. You might think I'm joking, but my sisters can attest that I do it, and it works! I don't know when I started, but at some point during the COVID-19 pandemic I started shouting out, "Come on, God . . . we know you can do it!" If I'm hoping for or dreaming of or wanting something, I take it to God directly and shout, "God, you can do it! Come on, God. We know you can do this!" God probably laughs at me, but I've felt really invigorated and God has definitely answered those prayers—er, pep talks. Sometimes God needs a little pep talk—don't we all? So give God pep talks! You'll love it and God will appreciate it.

Love more. Love deeper.

One of my favorite scripture passages is 1 Corinthians 13, the one that begins, "If I speak in the tongues of mortals and of angels, but do not have love, I am a noisy gong or a clanging cymbal. . ." I was really close to my grandfather—my mother's father. He asked to have this scripture read at his funeral, and ever since it's been my favorite. It's profound, yet simple: "Love is patient; love is kind. . ." Do everything in love—love more, love deeper. A quote often attributed to Mother Teresa goes, "Not all of us can do great things, but we can do small things with great love." So, whatever you do, every single day do every single thing with great love. Love more, love deeper.

Suffering can be a gateway to compassion and empathy.

I've said it before and I'll say it again—sometimes we go through what we go through so we can help others. Not that bad things need to happen to us—they really should not happen—but sometimes God uses those bad things to help others find their voice, their healing, their power. So, look for ways that you can use the things that have happened to you to help others. Suffering can open up a gateway to compassion and empathy, but it can also open up a gateway to our own freedom and a gateway for others to find their freedom. So, find healing, work through things you've endured and suffered (or are still suffering) in this life, and find freedom. You can help others break free of the shackles that this life has placed on their lives.

Choose victory over victimhood.

Every single day we face choices. We have the power to choose good over evil, light over darkness, and victory over victimhood. Our lives are a slew of circumstances and experiences—good and bad—but at the end of the day the power remains with us to be the victor or the victim of our own story. If you always choose victory over victimhood, you will give others courage and empower them, too, to be victors, not victims.

Believe that you can change the world and that your life has a purpose.

Your own life has the power to change the world. You—unique as your fingerprints—have a one-of-a-kind purpose. You are meant to be where you are, chosen, loved. Look at your life and see your unique gifts, talents, and purpose. Believe in that life, own it, and be it. You were made for greatness. You, and only you, were chosen to leave a special imprint on this world. Without you and your life this world would be missing so much. At this very moment you are living your legacy, you are writing history. Choose wisely. Don't miss a moment. Embrace who you are, who you were made to be! I can't wait to see what you do in this life and how you change the world by leaving your unique imprint on it.

Figure out who you were meant to be and LIVE IT OUT.

Some love her; some don't—although I don't know how anyone could dislike her. I've always loved Dolly Parton because she knows exactly who she is. She owns who she is, lives who she is. I love what Dolly says: "Find out who you are and do it on purpose." Find out who you are, who you were created to be. And every day, live that out. You have a purpose. God wants you to leave a unique mark on the people in your life, on this world. Find out who you were meant to be and live that out. Doing that, I assure you, will give others the passion, zeal, and courage to find out who they have been created to be and embrace the life that they were created for. By living our authentic lives we will change the world.

Let me leave you with a few simple words, a message that I hope you will tattoo on your heart: "You have been created for a purpose. You have been made for greatness. The world needs you, needs your life." Never forget. Every minute of every day your legacy, your story is being written. Embrace it.

New City Press

New City Press is one of more than 20 publishing houses sponsored by the Focolare, a movement founded by Chiara Lubich to help bring about the realization of Jesus' prayer: "That all may be one" (John 17:21). In view of that goal, New City Press publishes books and resources that enrich the lives of people and help all to strive toward the unity of the entire human family. We are a member of the Association of Catholic Publishers.

www.newcitypress.com
202 Comforter Blvd.
Hyde Park, New York

Periodicals
Living City Magazine
www.livingcitymagazine.com

Scan to join our mailing list for discounts and promotions or go to www.newcitypress.com and click on "join our email list."